Th

DIRECT MEANS

to

ETERNAL BLISS

by

Michael Langford

Previous editions published under the titles:

The Imposter

The Most Rapid and Direct Means to Eternal Bliss

The Most Direct Means to Eternal Bliss

www.theFreedomreligionpress.com

www.seeseer.com

ISBN: 978-1-937995-89-8

CONTENTS

INTRODUCTION

For thousands of years humans have been stuck in
the same pool of inward unsolved problems. Thousands of
years ago humans had the problems of suffering, sorrow,
anger, fear, violence, conning, cheating, lying, death, etc.
Today humans have the problems of suffering, sorrow,
anger, fear, violence, conning, cheating, lying, death, etc.
All of those problems have a single cause.
In this book the cause of the lack of progress and the
solution that actually works is revealed. There is a secret,
a missing link, a vicious circle, that is keeping humans
stuck in the same pool of unsolved problems.
That secret, that missing link, that vicious circle
is revealed in this book. How to break free
of that ancient human trap is also revealed in this book.
The solutions taught in the past have failed.
Not even one in a million humans has been freed from
all suffering and been established in absolutely perfect
infinite-eternal-awareness-love-bliss
by the solutions that have been taught in the past.
It is possible to be free of all sorrow and suffering
and to experience absolutely perfect infinite eternal joy
here and now in this lifetime.
It is possible for all humans, not just a few humans.
There is a rapid means to infinite bliss.
That rapid means is taught in this book.
Some of the strategies the ego uses to avoid Freedom
and how to end those strategies
are also revealed in this book.
Whatever spiritual path you are on,
this book can be a great help.
The problem of the ego distorting, distracting and keeping
the attention directed outward is a problem shared
by all humans, whatever path they are on.
The ego's tricks have seldom been looked at
in spiritual literature.

Some of the ego's tricks are revealed in this book.
How to put an end to the ego's tricks is also taught in this
book. The most direct and rapid means to end suffering
and sorrow and to live in awareness-love-bliss,
is of benefit to all.

HOW TO READ THIS BOOK

The purpose of an authentic spiritual teaching
is to awaken an experience. The purpose of an authentic
spiritual teaching is to awaken insight. To awaken insight,
read very slowly. Stay with one sentence for a very long
time before proceeding to the next sentence.

In this book the word ego refers to the false identity,
thought, the human mind, the impostor self.
Do not let the ego, which has misled humans
for as long as there have been humans,
prevent you from seeing what is being revealed
in this book.
This book contains only that which is most essential.

The ego controls thinking
and the ego does not like to be exposed.
Watch your thoughts to see how the ego tries to prevent
you from seeing what is being revealed in this book.
Do not allow the ego to distort
what is being revealed in this book.
Do not allow the ego to add to
what is being conveyed in this book,
for that too is a method the ego uses to distort.

The reason the spiritual teachings of the past
have failed to expose the tricks of the ego
and to bring the ego to a final end is because
the spiritual teachings of the past serve the ego.

This book is a step-by-step instruction manual.
This book is not for the purpose of
intellectual entertainment.
For human consciousness to be transformed,
something new must be introduced.
This book introduces something new
into human consciousness.

Infinite Love-Bliss is available in this lifetime.
It is possible to bring the impostor self to a final end.
What remains when the impostor self ends is
Infinite-Eternal-Awareness-Love-Bliss.

CHAPTER ONE

THE IMPOSTOR

The following definitions are only for the purpose of the teachings in this book. These are the definitions of the words *ego*, *Self* and *thought* that will be used in this book:
THOUGHT: Thoughts are the words of your language in your mind. If your native language is English and you write in English and speak English, those same English words in your mind are thoughts. Some people may speak, write and think in more than one language.
EGO: ego is the thought I. The ego is the "I thought." "I am happy." "I am sad." "I did this." "I did that." There are so many sentences in thought that contain the word "I." That thought "I" in each of those sentences is the ego. The ego is the idea of a separate, individual identity. The ego identifies with the body and with thought and calls the body and thought "I."
The ego is thought. The ego is thinking. Other words for the ego, as the word is being used in this book, are: impostor self, human mind, false self, false identity. There is far more to what the ego is than just thought, all that a human perceives is a part of the ego dream. However, for the purposes of this book the focus is on the ego as thought.

SELF: the Self (with a capital S) is infinite-eternal-awareness-love-bliss.
Those are five words pointing towards one-awareness.
Awareness-love-bliss are not three, they are one.
The Self is the background of awareness. Because almost all humans are in the habit of looking outward towards thoughts, the body, the world, people, places, things, etc., it *appears* as though the background of awareness (the Self) wakes up in the morning and goes to sleep at night.

If you turn your attention towards the background of
awareness, eventually you will discover:
the background of awareness is continuous.
Because almost all humans are in the habit of looking
outward towards thoughts, the body, the world, people,
places, things, etc., it *appears* as though
the background of awareness is limited.
If you turn your attention towards the awareness that
wakes up in the morning, instead of towards people,
places, things, thoughts, etc., eventually you will discover
that awareness is infinite-eternal-awareness-love-bliss.
The background of awareness that *appears* to wake up in
the morning is there during all the waking hours until one
goes to sleep at night. Thoughts come and go, but the
background of awareness that is aware of the thoughts
is there during all the waking hours and does not come
and go. The background of awareness is the true Self.
Technically one can say that the true Self is the
infinite Awareness and your background of awareness
is the doorway to that infinite awareness.

Before you learned the language you now think in,
the background of awareness was there. Then you learned
the word "I" in your language. Your body was given
a name and when people saw that body they said
"There goes John" (or Frank, or Jane, or Julie, or Kumar,
or Radha) or whatever name they gave your body.
Thus the idea arose "I am John, I am this body."
You existed as the background of awareness before that
I-thought arose. The thought calling its "self" "I"
is an impostor "self." The background of awareness is the
true Self. The fact that you existed before you learned
the language that became your thoughts helps to reveal
the difference between your true Self and the impostor.
Because you existed as the background of awareness
before you learned the language
that produced the thoughts you now think in,
you can easily see that the thought "I" is an impostor.
8

All thoughts are opposed to your real nature.
You know that thoughts are not part of your true nature
because you had to learn them. That is why you cannot
speak, write and think fluently in two hundred different
languages: because you have not acquired those languages.

You can observe that same process in an infant.
You can see that an infant is aware before it learns any
language. You can observe the child growing older and
learning a language. You can observe when the child
learns the word "I" and when the child begins to say the
word "I." Being able to see how the impostor arose in you
and how the impostor arises in every human infant
and child is a very important tool.
The reason it is a very important tool is:
you do not have to rely upon someone else to tell you
that the ego is an acquired impostor.
You can observe this for yourself.
Thought is something foreign, alien to the true Self.
Thought pretends to be the Self.
Thought is not the Self. Thought is an impostor.
Thought believes thought is a real entity
and thought believes thought is a real self.
Thought is not a real entity and thought is not a self.
Living from thought instead of living from Awareness
is the cause of all human suffering.
The impostor (thought – ego)
is the cause of all human problems, sorrow and suffering.
The background of awareness is the true Self.
The awareness, that *appears* to wake up in the morning,
is the true Self.
The awareness that *appears*
to be looking through your eyes now is the true Self.

As an example for clarification, you could view
thinking and memory as something like a computer
program. Within that computer program is a virus.
The virus is called the "I thought."

The virus controls the program.
The "I thought" controls all thinking.
The virus pretends to be your self.
The "I thought" pretends to be your self.
The virus creates tremendous sorrow and suffering.
The "I thought" creates tremendous sorrow and suffering.
None of the sorrow or suffering is needed.
What is needed is to delete the virus
that pretends to be your self.
What is needed is to delete the impostor self.

When one attempts to delete the virus,
the virus sends out many thoughts claiming
that deleting the virus is not a good idea.
The virus has many strategies
to preserve the illusion that it is real
and to continue the delusion that it is the real self.

In humans the program that came from the outside
and took control of their awareness
is called thought, language, and thinking.
In humans the virus is called the ego or the "I thought."
The "I thought" (ego) is an impostor pretending to be
the Self. The ego is the cause of all human sorrow and
suffering. The ego is the cause of all disease, death, war,
fear, anger and violence. Although many thousands of
years have passed, human beings have made almost no
inward progress toward ending suffering, sorrow, war,
fear, anger, violence, cheating and lying.
Thousands of years ago humans had suffering, sorrow,
war, fear, anger, violence, cheating and lying.
Now, today, currently, humans have suffering, sorrow,
war, fear, anger, violence, cheating and lying.
What has kept humans in the same pool
of inward unsolved problems?
The ego (the impostor) has kept humans in the same pool
of inward unsolved problems.
Inward problems cannot be solved by looking outward.
10

Inward problems can only be solved by looking inward.
The ego knows that if the attention is turned inward,
the ego will be found to be a myth, an impostor,
an illusion, a delusion, a dream.
Therefore, due to the ego's fear of ending,
the ego keeps the attention directed outward.
Usually when people attempt to turn the attention inward,
they are still looking outward because they do not
understand the meaning of looking inward.

All humans are slaves and the impostor "self" is
their master. Exposing the strategies of that impostor
"self", how to put an end to those strategies,
how to bring the impostor "self" to a final end,
thus ending all suffering and sorrow
and remaining in the true Self whose nature is
infinite-eternal-awareness-love-bliss,
are the primary purposes of this book.
Ending the ego does not end the body. After the ego ends,
the body will live out the natural course of its life.
One should never attempt to harm the body.
The ego is the "I thought." Ending the ego is ending the
"I thought." Ending the bodily life will not end the ego.
The ego will create the dream of a new body
when the old body ends.
Thus, ending the body does not help to solve the problems.

Humans almost always have their attention directed
outward towards thoughts, people, places, things,
experiences, etc. The background of awareness is
the true Self and humans almost always ignore it.
Your true Self deserves your attention.
When humans turn their attention *away* from thoughts,
the body, the world, people, places, things, experiences,
etc. and *towards* their awareness,
eventually they will directly experience their true Self.

The impostor (thought) pretending to be your Self and calling its pretend self "I" should not be tolerated even for one moment. Especially an impostor that has created so much suffering and sorrow should not be tolerated even for one moment. The impostor (thought) is like a parasite.

Because the ego believes it is a real entity, the ego is afraid of ending. The ego controls all thinking. Because the ego is afraid of ending and controls all thinking, the ego directs thought in ways that will preserve its imaginary self so that its imaginary self is not brought to an end.

The purpose of the teachings in this book is to bring the impostor to an end so that what remains is only the true Self whose nature is infinite-eternal-awareness-bliss-love. When the impostor ends, all suffering and sorrow also end.

Imagining that thinking or thought is your self is a delusion, a dreamlike illusion. Thinking that you are a body living in a world is a delusion, a dreamlike illusion. Thought has created those delusions.

All sorrow, suffering and delusions have one single root. The single root is thought. The root of thought is the "I thought." The root of thought is the thought "I."

Thought is not part of your true nature. Thought is something you learned. Do not allow something you acquired to pretend to be your self.

Try this experiment:
Set aside two hours
when you have no other activities going on.
Sit down in a place where you will not be disturbed.
Shut your eyes.
Make a decision that for the next two hours
you will not allow a single thought to arise.
If you are really in control of thinking,
then not even one thought will arise.
If thinking controls you,
then even though you have made the decision
not to allow a single thought to arise,
you will not be able to sit for two hours
without a single thought arising.
What a revelation this can be to discover that thought,
something that you acquired,
now controls you.

Chapter One contains a description of the secret
that has enslaved humanity
for as long as there have been humans.
Read Chapter One very slowly three times
before reading Chapter Two.

Some of the reasons for reading slowly and
repetitively are that people read spiritual books and
various self-improvement books, sometimes hundreds of
them, without any major change occurring in their lives.
One of the reasons for this is that
they are not familiar enough with the teachings
for the teachings to have become tools they can use.
In other words, the teachings have not really sunk in
after a single reading.
By reading one chapter three times
before going unto the next chapter
there is a much better chance of the teachings becoming
a useable tool that can actually transform one's life.

Since this book teaches
what the ego would prefer to block out,
this is even truer for this book.

It is an interesting experience to present a teaching,
have someone imagine something
about what they have read and then criticize the teaching
based on what they imagined,
which was not the teaching presented.

CHAPTER TWO

THE IMPOSTOR'S TRICKS

The ego controls all thinking. The ego can create
an argument against anything. Therefore, reserve all
arguments against what is being presented here until you
have read the book at least three times. Otherwise, the ego
will generate arguments against any anti-ego presentation,
thus blocking what is being presented.
See the vicious circle: The ego in its attempts to prevent
the ego from being exposed for the impostor that it is,
and to block the realization that the ego is the cause
of all human sorrow and suffering, creates arguments
against what is revealed in this book.
Because the ego sets the standards for the debate,
the ego always wins the debate.
The way to break that vicious circle is to delay
all arguments against what is presented here until
you have read the book very slowly at least three times.
Having the motivation to understand,
instead of the motivation to argue, will help to produce
an insight into what is being presented here.
At least give what is being presented here a fair chance
by being aware of the arguments that the ego creates
and disregarding those arguments
until an insight into what is revealed here is awakened.
Plenty of time to argue later, after reading the entire book.

The ego has been deceiving humans
for as long as there have been humans.
Be aware of the ego's attempts to deceive you.
The ego controls all thinking, therefore,
various combinations of thoughts, ideas, beliefs
and opinions are the ego's primary tools
to preserve the ego's imaginary "self"
and to prevent you from discovering your true Self.

Most humans have never observed
the background of awareness, not even for one second.
Therefore, whatever opinions most people have about
what the background of awareness is, what its qualities
are, what the true Self is, etc., have no basis.
If you observe the background of awareness
for many hours every day, for a number of years,
then you will eventually know that your awareness is
infinite-eternal-awareness-love-bliss. Because most
humans spend their entire lives looking outward at
thoughts, the body, the world, people, places, things, etc.,
most humans never observe their own awareness,
not even for one moment, in their entire lifetimes.

Concepts, beliefs and conclusions are not truly
important. What is truly important is Direct Experience.
Be aware of your thoughts, ideas, beliefs and opinions
and see how they serve the ego.
See Chapter One for a clarification
of the difference between the ego and the true Self.

This book is a practical guide to Direct Experience,
not a theory for intellectual entertainment.
Because the ego is afraid of ending, the ego directs and
creates thoughts, ideas, concepts, beliefs and opinions that
will help the ego to continue its illusion of being real and
that will prevent the ego from being brought to an end.
Those concepts are ego preservation strategies.
Those concepts are the ego's tricks. Because thoughts
can be combined in trillions of combinations,
the ego can create trillions of preservation strategies.
The ego has the ability to hide what it is doing from itself.
The ego creates ego preservation strategies throughout
the entire day. Most people are not aware of the ego's
preservation strategies. If you are not aware of how the
ego preserves its imaginary self, then the ego succeeds in
preserving its imaginary self. One of the purposes of this
book is to look at how the ego preserves its imaginary self.

If one million people study a spiritual teaching and only one of those people brings the ego illusion to its final end, why did the other nine hundred ninety-nine thousand, nine hundred ninety-nine miss the opportunity?
The reason the other nine hundred ninety-nine thousand nine hundred ninety-nine people missed the opportunity is because of the ego's fear of ending. Due to the ego's fear of ending, the ego creates strategies to preserve its imaginary self. Distorting spiritual teachings is one of the many strategies the ego uses to preserve its imaginary self.
That applies to the teachings in the book you are now reading and to all other spiritual teachings.

Right from the beginning, the ego's preservation strategies have to be dealt with.   If the ego's preservation strategies are not dealt with, the ego will block out or distort what is revealed in the book you are now reading.
Most attempts at awakening fail because of failure to put an end to the ego's preservation strategies.
The ego's preservation strategies can be brought to an end. We will look at how to do that in this book.
Usually any mention of exposing the ego's preservation strategies makes the ego run the other way.
Being willing to look at the ego's preservation strategies is a sign of spiritual maturity.
Most people are not willing to look at the ego's preservation strategies.
Reading a book that reveals some of the ego's preservation strategies will not make you immune to them.

One of the ego's preservation strategies is the thought "This does not apply to me."
The ego is very tricky and deceptive in all humans.
The ego is a liar in all humans.
The ego lies to its imaginary self.
When something is pointed out in this book and you think "This does not apply to me," take a second look.

Maybe it does apply to you and the ego is blocking that fact out as a preservation strategy. Challenge the thought "This does not apply to me." The thought "This does not apply to me" may be an ego preservation strategy.

One of the differences between the one out of millions who awakens and the others who do not is the ability to stay focused on an essential point until it becomes an insight and a tool that you can use. An intellectual understanding of what is revealed in this book is only the first step. The second step is to go beyond thought to awaken insight. The book you are now reading is filled with the insights that lay the foundation for you to be the one who awakens and not one of the millions who miss. Dwell on what is written in every sentence in every chapter until an insight is awakened that becomes a tool you can use. To awaken insight, don't read what is written here the way you read a newspaper or trivia, and don't read for the purpose of gathering information. To awaken insight, read as though you were reading instructions about how to fly that are vital to prevent you from crashing. Slowly reflect on each sentence. Continue to reread long after the intellect has understood the meaning of the words. Reading very, very slowly is insight reading. Read very slowly. Then read at an even slower pace, allowing you to look deeply into each sentence, and to see what each sentence points towards. The ego is like an inchworm that lets go of one thought only when it has grabbed hold of the next thought. Therefore, when rereading every chapter many times over and over, don't be in a hurry to proceed to the next sentence. Stay with each sentence for a long time before reading the next sentence.

It is important to understand the difference between insight and intellectual understanding.

Never confuse intellectual understanding with insight.
Intellectual understanding, which means understanding
the words, is good as a first step. However, after one has
understood the words, if one then goes on to another
concept before the insight has awakened, the words may
become obstacles and hindrances, instead of tools that
end the ego. Intellectual "understanding", an intellectual
appetite and an intellectual approach to "spirituality" are
what characterize the nine hundred ninety-nine thousand
nine hundred ninety-nine who miss.
Insight is the approach used by the one out of millions
who brings the ego to its final end.
Most people study "spiritual" teachings
because they enjoy the concepts.
The ego is fundamentally dishonest in humans and the ego
has the ability to hide what it is doing from its imaginary
"self." Therefore, many people fail to see that their
primary reason for studying "spiritual" teachings
is because they enjoy the concepts.
The desire to go quickly to the next concept and to gather
more and more information and to read more and more
spiritual books and to think about what has been read
and to discuss what has been read and thought about,
are symptoms of the intellectual appetite
and intellectual "spirituality".
Approaching the study of spiritual teachings intellectually,
as just described, is an approach used by the nine hundred
ninety-nine thousand nine hundred ninety-nine who miss.

No opinions, philosophies or beliefs are presented in
this book. The report of Direct Experience and a practical
guide to Direct Experience are presented in the book you
are now reading. Ideas are not what this book
points towards. This book points towards
the awareness that is prior to thought,
and how to directly experience that awareness.

The ego likes to scatter attention.

Scattering attention is one of the ego's preservation strategies. Thinking scatters attention.
To bring the attention to a single point
and to dwell on that single point for a very long time
is the way to awaken insight.
Insight is not thinking and insight is not belief.
Insight is a permanent new perspective.

To find one powerful quote, not a quote that the spiritually immature ego selects in its efforts to preserve itself, and to stay with that quote until insight awakens, is the kind of approach used by the one in millions
who brings the ego to its final end.
Those who use this approach are rare.

Keeping the attention directed outward is one of the ego's fundamental tricks. Creating unnecessary activities is one way the ego keeps the attention directed outward and is another of the ego's tricks.
Dropping all unnecessary activities to create the maximum amount of time for spiritual practice is an essential key to success in bringing the ego to its final end.

Pretending that a journey through thought
is an authentic spiritual journey
is also one of the ego's tricks.
The ego has as many tricks to draw upon as there are concepts, ideas, beliefs and opinions. Choosing belief instead of Direct Experience is one of the ego's tricks.

Wasting time is one of the ego's tricks.
Spending time in entertainment that could have been spent in spiritual practice is one of the ego's tricks.
Almost all thoughts are just the ego's tricks.

Reflect on one sentence for a very long time
before reading the next sentence.
Reflecting means looking.

Reflecting does not mean thinking
and reflecting does not mean arguing.

Stay with each sentence until you have an insight
into it. The previous sentence describes a key approach
used by the one in millions who succeeds
in living in infinite-eternal-awareness-love-bliss.

There are a few key principles to be understood
and a little reading may be required for that.
However, to go on and on reading
more and more spiritual books,
one after another,
is an ego preservation strategy;
another trick the ego uses.

Most reading, discussing
and thinking about spiritual teachings
are ego preservation strategies
(tricks created by the ego to preserve its imaginary self).
The ego continues thinking about spiritual concepts
to avoid the practice that leads to the ego's final end.
The ego keeps people lost in an endless maze of concepts.
Spiritual concepts do not lead to Freedom.

Only practice leads to Freedom.
However, it must be the most rapid and direct
spiritual practice and not a practice created by
or distorted by the ego.

Read Chapter Two very slowly three times
before reading Chapter Three. For quotes that support
the teachings in this book read the book *The Seven Steps
to Awakening*. There is more information about *The
Seven Steps to Awakening* on the last page of this book.
The Seven Steps to Awakening is a collection of quotes by
Seven Liberated Sages. *The Seven Steps to Awakening*
works very well with the book you are now reading.

CHAPTER THREE

THE IMPOSTOR'S TOOLS:

THOUGHT, THINKING AND BELIEFS

Thought is the primary tool the ego uses to preserve its imaginary self. Therefore, it is important to see how the ego uses thought to create ego preservation strategies. First one must understand the nature of thinking, thought, concepts and beliefs and the myths the ego has created about thinking, thought, concepts and beliefs.
Thought is not a means to discover the absolute Truth. The ego has convinced almost all humans and almost all spiritual aspirants that thought is a means to know the absolute Truth. Some people think they already know that thought is not a means to know the absolute Truth. Almost all of those people are still trying to use thought as a means to know the absolute Truth. This reveals that they do *not* really know that thought is not a means to know the absolute Truth. They have confused knowing-insight-awareness with conceptual "knowing."

People tend to believe in thought. Thinking is controlled by the ego and the ego uses thought to preserve its imaginary self. Therefore, to believe in thoughts, ideas and concepts, including those thoughts that people imagine are their own thoughts, is an error that results in failure to end the ego. Thoughts, ideas, beliefs, concepts, emotions and desires are the fundamental tools the impostor self (ego) uses to prevent you from directly experiencing your True Self. For those few individuals who are seriously intent on Freedom, it is essential to stop using thought as a means to know the absolute Truth.

It is also essential to stop believing in thoughts, ideas, and concepts; including those thoughts, ideas and concepts you imagine being your own. Understanding the nature of beliefs can help one to see that thought is not a means to know the absolute Truth. *Seeing* that thought is not a means to know the absolute Truth is a way to stop using thought as a means to know the absolute Truth.

There is a method you can try that reveals that thought is not a means to know the absolute Truth. It is the "How Do You Know Method." Here are the instructions for the How Do You Know Method: Look at any belief you have. Ask of that belief, *"How do I know absolutely for sure this is true?"* The mind will give an answer. To the answer the mind gives ask *"How do I know absolutely for sure this is true?"* Every time the mind gives an answer, question the answer by repeating the question *"How do I know absolutely for sure this is true?"* You must be willing to question *every* answer the mind gives for the method to work. If you are willing to question *every* answer the mind gives to the question *"How do I know absolutely for sure this is true?"* the inquiry will always end in "I don't know absolutely for sure this is true". The How Do You Know Method is an excellent way to see the difference between believing and knowing. The How Do You Know Method is also an excellent way to see that thought is not a means to know the absolute Truth. After questioning a few hundred beliefs using the How Do You Know Method, it should be quite clear that thought is not a means to know the absolute Truth. Thought is like a great pretense or house of cards. One idea is supported by another idea. One assumption supports another assumption. The How Do You Know Method is a way to see that when you trace each idea back, you find there is actually no real foundation at all.

There is another way to see that thought is not a way
to know the absolute Truth: understand the nature of
belief and concepts; see how belief is formed and
how the ego creates ideas that preserve its imaginary self.
It is the "Arguing Both Sides Method". The Arguing Both
Sides Method begins by looking at some belief you have,
maybe one of the current issues of the day.
Write an argument for your belief. Look at your belief and
write up all the proofs, arguments, evidence, and reasons
that support it. Next, pretend that you have the opposite
belief and write up all the proofs, arguments, evidence
and reasons that support that opposite belief.
The purpose of the Arguing Both Sides Method
is to demonstrate that thought can create reasons,
evidence and support for any belief. Seeing that thought
can create evidence and reasons to support any belief
is a very powerful key. The Arguing Both Sides Method
is another way of revealing that thought is really baseless.

The Arguing Both Sides Method also demonstrates
that thought forms conclusions based on motive.
Evidence is not the primary factor that determines
what conclusions and beliefs will be formed.
Motivation is the primary factor in the forming of beliefs.
Evidence will be gathered to support the motive.
The ego will gather all the so-called evidence and reasons
to support what the ego wants to believe.

The ego's primary motive
is to preserve its imaginary self.
Therefore, the ego directs thought to create concepts
that will help to preserve its imaginary self.
In almost all humans, including almost all spiritual
aspirants and students, the desire of the ego
to preserve its imaginary self is very strong.
In almost all humans including almost all spiritual
aspirants and students, the ego directs thought
to create concepts that will preserve its imaginary self.
24

One of the ego's preservation strategies is selecting spiritual paths that are not direct. Even if one manages to find the Direct Path, the ego will distort the Direct Path by interpreting what is written or said in a way that supports the ego, or the ego will distort the Direct Path by focusing on that which is not essential.

One of the tricks (ego preservation strategies) that the ego uses most commonly with spiritual aspirants is to confuse intellectual "spirituality" with authentic spirituality. Most people only have an intellectual interest in spiritual concepts and do not wish to end the ego. Most people just enjoy learning about the concepts. There are some people who realize their interest is only intellectual. There are other people who believe they have an interest in ending the ego, who do not really have an interest in ending the ego. Almost all of the people on a spiritual path that claims to have as its aim the ending of the ego illusion, have very little desire to end the ego illusion. The way to end all of the ego's preservation strategies is to increase the desire for Freedom.

There are a few very condensed Direct Path teachings that can be a great help on the Direct Path. You will find those Direct Path teachings in the book you are now reading, and in the book *The Seven Steps to Awakening* and in a few other books. However, to go on and on reading books and discussing spiritual teachings is an ego preservation strategy to keep you in the realm of thought instead of practice. A time will come when your time would be better spent doing direct spiritual practice instead of endless reading. *Practice* leads to Freedom.
Endless reading and discussing leads to illusion.

The ego creates arguments against the Direct Path as a preservation strategy. The ego calls indirect paths "direct paths" as an ego preservation strategy.

Instead of spending all one's spare time in spiritual practice, the ego finds almost endless ways to spend one's spare time, and this is one of the ego's primary preservation strategies. Some examples of this are television, entertainment, reading, discussing, and thinking. The ego can find thousands of ways to avoid spiritual practice.
If you drop all of your unnecessary activities, you will have much more time for spiritual practice.

One ego preservation strategy (one of the impostor's tricks) is creating arguments against what is written here instead of open-mindedly considering the possibility that what is revealed in this book points towards the truth that the ego prevents most people from seeing. Another ego preservation strategy (trick the impostor uses) is deciding in advance that one of the methods will not work, without ever giving the method a sincere try.

See how the ego directs every thought to create a way to preserve its imaginary self. In other words, ask of every thought, idea, concept, belief, etc.:
"*Does this thought, idea, concept or belief help the ego illusion to continue?*"
When the mind answers that question "no" just assume that is another ego lie.
The human mind has thousands of layers of self deception.
A lie behind a lie behind another lie.

When you form a belief, you are no closer to discovering the absolute Truth than you were before you formed the belief. When you form a belief, you have created an obstacle to discovering the absolute Truth.
If you were honest, instead of a belief, your view would be "I don't know." If you really wanted Truth, you would insist on Direct Experience.
If you really wanted Truth, you would never accept a belief.
A belief is only a group of symbols. All words are symbols.
26

The extremely intense desire for Freedom
is the key to ending the ego's tricks, and the book
you are now reading contains step-by-step instructions
for awakening the extremely intense desire for Freedom.

This book exposes some of the strategies the ego
uses to preserve its imaginary self. Reading this book is a
good first step. Repeated reading, over and over, reflecting
on each sentence, is very important. If at some point in
the future you have dropped all unnecessary activities and
are using all of the free time thus created to practice the
Awareness Watching Awareness Method, or the Abandon
Release Method, or the Loving Consciousness Method
then your time would be far better spent in practice
instead of reading. However, in the beginning, most
people need a foundation to motivate them to drop all
unnecessary activities and to practice, and thus in the
beginning reading this book is very important. Repetition,
reading the same chapter over and over has great value.
Such repetition helps to penetrate those
thousands of layers of human self deception.
Such repetition helps one to remember the teachings
so that they can become tools that one can use.

Your motivation while reading is very important.
The correct motivations are:
*Extremely intense Self-honesty.
*An extremely intense desire to directly experience
the infinite-eternal-absolute Truth.
*A willingness to let go of all the ideas
you have accumulated in the past.
*An extremely intense longing to be free of suffering
and sorrow and to live in eternal-joy.

If the extremely intense desire for Freedom
is awakened in you, it will bring clarity, honesty, insight,
integrity and earnestness.

When the extremely intense desire for Freedom
is awakened, clarity, sincerity, earnestness, insight
and discernment are also awakened, and then you can *see*
what is essential and what is not essential.

 The end of the ego
is the end of all suffering and all sorrow for all eternity.
The end of the ego is infinite-eternal-awareness-love-bliss.
Realize that ending the ego is the only truly worthwhile
event that can happen in a human life.
Take a *look* at your actions moment by moment
to *see* if they conform to the realization that ending the ego
is the only truly valuable event
that can happen in a human life.

 The ego projects thoughts and fantasies
and the ego interprets.
One way to stop this distortion is to ask,
"Is this thought I am having about what I am reading
really in the words I am reading,
or have I added a thought
that is not there in the words I am reading?"
Another way to stop the distortion is to ask,
"Have I added a concept or interpretation
to what I am reading?" Repeat these questions often.
Actually put what is written above into practice.
Most people project much thinking onto the teachings
that they read. Their thinking has very little to do with the
teachings they have read. Almost all humans are in a state
of chaotic confusion. Most people do not realize that they
are in a state of chaotic confusion. Interpreting what is
written is an expression of that chaotic confusion.
Awakening the extremely intense desire for Freedom
will stop the ego from creating ego preservation strategies.
Chapter Four is about the importance of awakening
the extremely intense desire for Freedom.
Read Chapter Three very slowly three times
before reading Chapter Four.

CHAPTER FOUR

THE DESIRE FOR FREEDOM

Awakening the extremely intense desire for
Freedom is the most important first step that can be taken
towards being liberated now in this lifetime.
Awakening the extremely intense desire for Freedom
is the most important key in the book you are now reading.
Awakening the extremely intense desire for Freedom
is the foundation for Freedom.

The extremely intense desire for Freedom is:
*The extremely intense desire
for the direct experience of the absolute Truth.
*The extremely intense longing
for the final end of all suffering and sorrow.
*The extremely intense desire
to experience eternal-love-joy.
*The extremely intense desire
to experience who or what you really are at your core
and to live eternally as your true Self.
*The extremely intense desire for Freedom from all
illusion and delusion and Freedom from the ego (impostor
self) which is the source of all illusion and delusion.
*The extremely intense desire
to awaken from the human nightmare.

The extremely intense desire for Freedom is
the foundation of all true spirituality. Of all of the factors
that determine if you will or will not be free,
the intensity or lack of intensity of your desire for Freedom
is the most essential factor.
Whatever you can do to most effectively increase
your desire for Freedom should be done.
Spiritual teachings are not all equal.
Some teachings are essential powerful keys.

The knowledge that increasing your desire for Freedom
is the most effective first step you can take is an essential
powerful key. All obstacles that appear in your journey
to Freedom are caused by too little desire for Freedom.
Even a little increase in your desire for Freedom is helpful.
As your desire for Freedom grows in intensity,
the ego creates fewer obstacles.
When your desire for Freedom becomes very intense,
your desire for Freedom demands
that you take no detours.

When your desire for Freedom becomes extremely
intense, for the first time you can see what is essential for
Freedom and what is not essential. When your desire for
Freedom is weak, the ego does not allow you to see its
preservation strategies. When the desire for Freedom
is stronger, you can begin to see the ego's preservation
strategies. When the desire for Freedom becomes even
stronger, the desire for Freedom itself will bring you
everything you need to succeed in your quest for Freedom
including the answer to all your questions, the Direct Path
teachings, the solution to all obstacles, the motivation to
practice, etc. You will be able to see how before the
awakening of the extremely intense desire for Freedom,
the ego selected spiritual teachings that would help to
preserve the ego. When the desire for Freedom becomes
even more intense you can see all of the ego's preservation
strategies. When the extremely intense desire for Freedom
is awakened you will marvel at how it was possible you did
not see the ego's preservation strategies before. When
the extremely intense desire for Freedom is awakened,
you will be able to see how the ego distorted even the
Direct Path teachings. When the extremely intense desire
for Freedom is awakened, you will be able to see that every
spiritual teaching from the past has been distorted by the
ego and that some of the spiritual teachings were created
by the ego for the purpose of preserving the ego.

When the extremely intense desire for Freedom is
awakened, you will be able to see that almost all
of the spiritual and religious teachings of the past
are distractions and detours that serve the ego. When the
extremely intense desire for Freedom is awakened, you
will be surprised at how little the ego let you see before.
When the extremely intense desire for Freedom is
awakened, you will see the endless maze of concepts
the ego created to trap your attention.
When the desire for Freedom becomes even more intense,
the ego will no longer create ego preservation strategies.
The extremely intense desire for the direct experience of
the absolute Truth will guide you to your inner Teacher.
The extremely intense desire for Truth will guide you to
the practice that gives the direct experience of Eternal Life.
The key is the intensity of the desire for the direct
experience of the absolute Truth. Increasing your desire
for the Truth is the most important first step.
Increasing your desire for Freedom is essential.

　　　　Without an increase in your desire for Freedom,
all of your attempts at awakening
will fail to produce the Eternal Experience.
Without an increase in your desire for Freedom,
the ego will distort all of your spiritual studies,
including what you read in this book.
Without an increase in your desire for Freedom,
the ego will never allow you to see the Truth.

　　　　Another great key is Self-honesty.
Self-honesty will help in all aspects of the quest for
Freedom. Self-honesty will help you increase your desire
for Freedom. Self-honesty is being as honest as you can
be. Self-honesty means to be 100% honest with your Self,
all the time. Catch your ego using ego preservation
strategies. See your ego creating arguments, reasons,
excuses and concepts that lead you away from the
Direct Path.

What if your desire for Freedom were to double
from its present level? If your desire for Freedom were to
double from its present level, that would be a huge help.
If your desire for Freedom were to double from its present
level, immediately you would begin to see
what you have never been able to see before.
What if your desire for Freedom were a million times
greater and more intense than it is now?
Really, even if your desire for Freedom doubles or triples,
great changes will occur in what the ego allows you to see.
When your desire for Freedom increases greatly,
every moment of your life will be dedicated to your
Freedom. That great intense desire for Freedom will
demand that you do not waste even one moment of time,
that you stop the ego lies,
and that you drop that which is not essential.
The wonderful thing is, that same extreme desire for
Freedom that brings you the knowledge of what is
essential and what is not essential,
also allows you to see for the first time in your life.
Before the extremely intense desire for Freedom arises,
you think you can see, but really you are blind.
After the extremely intense desire for Freedom arises
all is made clear and you have no doubts!
After the extremely intense desire for Freedom arises,
for the first time you can see!

        If the extremely intense desire for Freedom
does *not* arise in you:
*The words in this book will be of little
or no real benefit to you.
*The ego will interpret what is written here.
*The ego will create arguments
against what is written here.
*Instead of seeing what you read literally,
without any interpretation,
the ego will begin to interpret.

*The ego will change the teachings
into something that preserves the ego
instead of something that brings the ego to its final end.

Therefore, the most essential key
is to awaken the extremely intense desire for Freedom
and to make that desire for Freedom grow every day.
If the desire for Freedom is not great enough in you,
the ego will always find a way to occupy your time
with something other than spiritual practice.
Thus the key to bringing the ego to an end
is the intensity of the desire for Freedom.

Imagine someone being held underwater.
How eager is he to rise to the surface to breathe air?
Your desire for Freedom must be as intense as that man's
desire for air. Freedom must be as high on your list
of priorities as air is on that man's list of priorities.
How great and how intense is the desire for air
for someone being held underwater?
He (or she) would like to rise to the surface,
but he is being held underwater. See how intense
his desire is to rise to the surface so he can breathe air.
Every second his desire to rise to the surface becomes
more and more intense. After one minute underwater,
his desire to breathe is much more intense.
After two minutes underwater, his desire
to rise to the surface for oxygen is ten times greater.
After three minutes underwater, his desire
to rise to the surface is one hundred times greater.
After four minutes underwater, his desire
to rise to the surface is one thousand times greater.
How great and how intense is his desire?
That is how great and how intense your desire for Freedom
must become, if you are going to succeed
in your quest for Eternal Freedom.
If the extremely intense desire for Freedom is not present,
you can always find a way to avoid spiritual practice.

33

If the extremely intense desire for Freedom is not present, there is almost no limit to the ego's capacity to distort. Suppose there was a book written by an awakened sage that was one thousand pages long and the only words that were written were the following identical words repeated on every page:

"The only effective means to end the ego illusion is to turn your attention away from thought, the body, the world, people, places, things, experiences, etc., and turn your attention towards awareness watching awareness.
If through other means you attempt to bring the ego to an end, the ego may appear to have ended; however, eventually the ego will reappear. Therefore, there are no other effective means to end the ego, to end all suffering and all sorrow, and to live eternally as infinite-awareness-love-bliss. Start by setting aside at least two hours per day, with no other activities, for your practice of awareness watching awareness.
If by dropping unnecessary activities you can create more than two hours for practice, do so.
Set aside as many hours per day as you can spare to practice awareness watching awareness, with no other activities occurring during your practice time."

Even if the above paragraph was written on every page, most people would not put into practice the instructions given in those verses. Most people would not put the instructions into practice because their desire for Freedom is not strong enough. The desire to preserve the ego is much greater than the desire to end the ego. This is true for almost all humans and almost all spiritual aspirants. The ego has trillions of tricks to preserve its imaginary self. To the previously quoted paragraph the aspirant might say: "He does not really mean the only effective means." "He does not really mean we need to set aside time with no other activities." "He does not really mean we need to practice." "The book is actually written in code."

34

"There are deeper, hidden, subtle meanings
that are more important."
If this seems insane to you, you are correct, it is insane.
The word "insane" describes almost all humans.
They may not use those exact words
to distort and complicate.
They will find their own words to distort and complicate.
The truth is he really does mean the only effective means;
and that time must be set aside for practice
with no other activities; and that you need to practice.
He really wrote in plain words without a code;
and he really wanted you to take the words literally
without searching for hidden meanings.

The only cure for all this is the awakening
of the extremely intense desire for Freedom.
What if your present desire for Freedom were to become
a million times more intense than it is now?:
*Then there would not be time for all these games,
detours, distractions, delays and distortions.
*Then you would stop listening to teachers
who are supposedly liberated but who are not liberated.
*Then you would not pretend that thinking about
spirituality is authentic Spirituality.
*Then you would not pretend that an intellectual journey
is a Spiritual journey.
*Then the only means you would accept
is the most direct means.

Then you would be just like the man
who is being held underwater trying to rise up for air:
*He does not have time for discussion.
*He does not have time for games.
*He does not have time for false teachers.
*He does not have time for indirect methods.
*He does not have time for endless reading.
*He does not have time for television.

*He does not have time for projecting
an imagined meaning onto the teachings.
*He does not have time for entertainment.
*He does not have time for pretending to want to be free.
*He does not have time for any dishonesty with himself.
*He does not have time for pretending
he has risen to the surface.
*He does not have time for any debate or argument.

The only problem an aspirant ever has is
a desire for Freedom that is too weak.
An extremely intense desire for Freedom
will solve all the other problems.

Read Chapter Four very slowly three times
before reading Chapter Five.

CHAPTER FIVE

HOW TO AWAKEN

THE EXTREMELY INTENSE

DESIRE FOR FREEDOM

The primary means to awaken
the extremely intense desire for Freedom
is to carefully examine these two choices every day
until the extremely intense desire for Freedom awakens:
Choice A is to choose to end the ego (the impostor self)
by dropping all unnecessary activities to create
the maximum amount of time every day to practice
the most direct and rapid means to eternal bliss.
The most direct and rapid means to eternal bliss
is the Awareness Watching Awareness Method
described in Chapter Seven.
Choice A is Infinite-Eternal-Awareness-Love-Bliss
with no sorrow and no suffering.
Choice A is Eternal Life.
Choice A is to live as your true Self forever.
Choice A is absolutely perfect joy.
The above is a summary of Choice A.

Some people may find it helpful to read more
descriptions of Choice "A" written by the Awakened Ones
who have taught in the past.
The Step Two and Step Five quotes in the book
The Seven Steps to Awakening describe Choice A.

Choice B is being identified with a body
subject to suffering, disease, death, violence, anger, fear,
etc. Choice B is to allow an impostor called the ego
to pretend to be yourself and to control you.

Choice B is to allow an impostor (ego) that has created
all the wars, diseases, death, suffering and evil
that every human has ever experienced, to continue.
Choice B is to have a temporary and therefore futile life
that leads only to death. That is a summary of Choice B.

In order to better examine Choice B you can make
a list of all the forms that human suffering takes.
You can write on that list thousands of wars; thousands of
diseases; thousands of forms of violence; all of the ways
that humans deceive, hurt, and cheat each other; and
every other form of human suffering that you can think of.
Usually humans look at only a small part of the ocean of
human suffering. The purpose of the list is to look at the
entire ocean of human suffering and the entire negative
side of human life in a single glance. The purpose
of the list is to see the consequences of choosing B.
You need only read the suffering list once.
After that, repeated reading of the summaries of choices A
and B in Chapter Five should be enough.
Read Chapter Five every day comparing the summary
of Choice A and the summary of Choice B until
the extremely intense desire for Freedom awakens in you.
Read Chapter Five everyday until you Choose A.

An aid to awakening the extremely intense desire
for Freedom is to see the value of the Eternal and the
futility of the temporary. The ego leads humans
throughout their lives from one temporary trivial pursuit
to another temporary trivial pursuit.
To see the pointlessness of the temporary
and the great value of the Eternal can be a great help.
If you look into the future to see where all these trivial
pursuits and useless activities will lead in the end,
that also can be a great aid in revealing
the pointlessness of the temporary.
Actually apply and practice the following questions:
(On top of page 39).

Ask of each activity and each moment,
"What does this lead to?", and after that "Then what?"
and later, "What will this finally lead to in the end?"

Often remembering that the body
can end at any moment can also help to awaken
the extremely intense desire for Freedom.
Living every day as though it is your last day,
using each precious moment to prepare for the Eternal,
can also be a great help.
Imagine there are two businesses you could invest in.
You can see that a wrecking ball is about to destroy the
first business. You can see that the second business will
last forever. The obvious wise choice is to invest
in the business that will last forever.
So it is with the choice between Eternal and temporary life.

How will you know you have made Choice A?
When you drop all unnecessary activities every day
and use all of that free time to practice every day
the most direct and rapid means to eternal bliss.
How will you know the extremely intense
desire for Freedom has been awakened?
When you drop all unnecessary activities every day and
use all of the free time thus created to actually practice
every day the most direct and rapid means to eternal bliss,
you will know the extremely intense desire for Freedom
has been awakened.

The Awakening
of the extremely intense desire for Freedom,
which can also be called "really making Choice A," is:
*Like a sign a trillion miles high stating NO MORE.
*NO MORE to all of the human evils of the past.
*NO MORE to all of the horrors the ego has created.
*Like a silent shout saying NO MORE so loudly
that if it were given a voice
it would shatter the eardrums of every human on earth.

*A demand for Truth.
*The absolute demand for absolute Truth.
*The absolute demand
for the final end of all human opinions.
*The absolute demand for absolute goodness.
*The absolute demand
for the final end of the impostor who is called ego.
*The absolute demand
for the Direct Experience of the true Self.
*Like an infinitely strong grip that grabs hold of Truth
with a power so strong nothing can weaken it.
*Like an infinitely strong grip
that grabs hold of the true Self with such strength,
nothing is powerful enough to weaken that grip.
*Like an infinitely strong grip that grabs hold of
the absolute goodness that has never known falsehood
with a hold so strong that nothing can weaken that grip.
*Like an absolutely immovable "NO"
saying no to the trillions of human lies spoken in the past
and the billions of human lies being thought of each day.
*Like an absolute "NO" to the trillions of horrors
humans have created in the past
and the billions of horrors humans are creating every day.
*An absolute demand
for the end of all sorrow and suffering.
*An absolute demand for perfect infinite-eternal-love-joy.
*An absolute demand that the source of all suffering,
violence and evil, which is the impostor called ego,
comes to a final end.
*An absolute devotion to the true Self
that is the background of awareness.
*An absolute devotion that is turning the attention
away from the world, the body, thought, etc.,
and towards awareness watching awareness.
*A demand for Truth that never compromises.
*A demand for the end of thought.
*A demand for the direct experience of the absolute Truth.

When the extremely intense desire for Freedom
arises, these demands are directed inwards,
not towards others.
When the extremely intense desire for Freedom arises,
one never again bows before any egotistical human.
When the extremely intense desire for Freedom arises,
all obstacles are swept away.
The extremely intense desire for Freedom
is absolute dedication and devotion to the absolute Truth.
It is absolute dedication and devotion
to knowing the true Self in direct experience.

After the extremely intense desire for Freedom
is awakened, every moment of one's life is dedicated to
awakening from the human dream. When the extremely
intense desire for Freedom is awakened, all of the ego's
lies, tricks, deceptions and games are seen for what they
are and all of the ego's lies, tricks, deceptions and games
eventually end. When
the extremely intense desire for Freedom is awakened,
the nightmare the ego has created is no longer tolerated.

The ego is the source of all evil. The ego is insane.
This is true for all humans. To produce so many
trillions of horrors, the ego has to be evil and insane.

Something in you longs for
an end to the impostor's dream.
Something in you longs for infinite Love.
Something in you longs for
the end of all suffering and sorrow.
Something in you longs for eternal-joy-love.

It is possible to end the ego's dream
and to discover the true Self which is free of all suffering
and whose nature is infinite-eternal-love-joy.
It is possible in this lifetime while this body is living.
Cooperate with your Heart. Stop listening to your ego.

If you turn your attention away from thought and towards awareness watching awareness and sustain that look for many hours every day, eventually the ego dream will end and the true Self will be experienced.
Then all suffering ends and what remains is the eternal perfection of awareness-love-bliss.

Make Choice A. Make your choice absolute and absolutely immovable. Make your choice absolutely solid and final. Your true Self, the background of awareness that is looking through your eyes, deserves your attention. For your entire life, you have been ignoring your true Self. Your true Self, the background of awareness, deserves your love and attention. Demand sanity. The human dream is insane. Demand sanity by waking up from the human dream into the reality of your own awareness.
Make Choice A by dropping all unnecessary activities to create more time for spiritual practice.
Make Choice A by dropping all distractions, detours and entertainment to create more time every day for spiritual practice.
Make Choice A by making sure your practice is the most direct and rapid means to eternal bliss.

The suffering that life brings is also a means to awaken the extremely intense desire for Freedom. Reading Chapter Five in *The Direct Means to Eternal Bliss* and the Step Five quotes in *The Seven Steps to Awakening* everyday is a much easier means to awaken the extremely intense desire for Freedom.

Some people will have an insight that permanently awakens the extremely intense desire for Freedom. However, for most people the awakening of the extremely intense desire for Freedom is a daily battle, with the intensity of the desire for Freedom fluctuating. Read Chapter Five very slowly at least three times before reading Chapter Six.

CHAPTER SIX

THE

AWARENESS WATCHING AWARENESS

DISCOVERY

By the year 2001 the author of the book you
are now reading had been studying the teachings of almost
all of the various religions and spiritual paths for 27 years.
He had read more than two thousand spiritual books.
He had received instruction from many spiritual teachers
in America and India.
It was clear that the essence of most spiritual teachings
was focusing the attention on the "I AM."
The place where "Hinduism," Buddhism, Judaism,
Christianity and Islam meet is turning inward
and focusing the attention on "I AM."
The most direct and rapid means to eternal bliss,
finding the kingdom within, "Self-Realization," Nirvana,
etc., is turning the attention within to focus on "I AM."

One modern example of this in "Hinduism" is
Sri Nisargadatta Maharaj. Nisargadatta's teacher (guru)
told him to pay attention to the "I AM" to the exclusion of
all else. Nisargadatta practiced focusing his attention on
the "I AM" for three years. After three years of practicing
in his spare time, Nisargadatta realized his true Self.
Nisargadatta had to work to support his family;
therefore, he could only practice in his spare time.
He spent hours each day looking at the true Self.
Focusing the attention on "I AM,"
excluding all else from one's attention,
is an ancient "Hindu" practice.

In Zen Buddhism
focusing the attention on "who is looking"
is found in the teachings of Master Bassui.
In Tibetan Buddhism focusing attention on awareness
is found in some of the Dzogchen practice instructions.

The importance of looking inward and knowing
the "I AM" is also found in the Judeo-Christian teachings:
"And God said to Moses, I AM THAT I AM. And He said
Thus you shall say to the children of Israel, I AM has sent
me to you." (Exodus 3:14) "Be still and know I AM God."
(Psalm 46:10). The entire book *The Impersonal Life*,
a book of Christian Mysticism, is written around
the single verse "Be still and know I AM God."
"Jesus said, Before Abraham was, I AM." (John 8:58)
"Jesus said, The Kingdom of God is within you."
(Luke 17:21). Jesus did *not* say, "*Will be* within you *after*
your body dies." Jesus said "is." "Is" is present tense.
"Is" is now.

The Prophet Mohammad said, "He who knows his
Self knows his Lord." Self-Cognition is a Sufi practice.
There are many other spiritual traditions and teachings
that have pointed out that focusing the attention on the
"I AM" is the most direct and rapid means to Freedom
(i.e. Know thyself).

Another modern example from "Hinduism"
is Sri Ramana Maharshi. Ramana Maharshi taught
for more than 50 years that the only effective means to
end the ego and suffering and to remain as eternal joy
is to focus on the Self, the I, the I AM.

By the year 2001, the author of the book you are
now reading had attempted to practice the method of
focusing the attention on the "I AM" for 27 years.
The author had made very little progress with that method
or any other method.

In December of 2001 the author was in Tiruvannamalai, India for the purpose of attending the talks of a teacher in the Ramana Maharshi tradition. The author was alone in a room at the Sesha Bhavan guesthouse. The author was thinking about all the possible meanings of "I" and "I AM" and all the possible approaches to "I" and "I AM" that he had read about over the years: The "I thought," the thought I AM. The "I feeling," the feeling I AM. The "I consciousness," the "I AM" consciousness. To think I or I AM. To feel I or I AM. To focus the attention on I or I AM. Many different combinations of approaches and the different views of what "I" or "I AM" means.

After 27 years, the author was still not sure what "I AM" means in direct experience. The author was wondering if there was some way to solve these questions and to have clarity both in the meaning of I or I AM and how to approach it; whether to focus the attention on I AM, or feel I AM, or think I AM, or...? The author wanted an understanding that was so clear, there would be nothing vague remaining, no more choices remaining. The author really wanted to know the answer. The author was not going to confine the answer to any previous understanding. The author was willing to have his previous understanding shattered, if necessary. There was a willingness to consider the possibility that for the last two and a half decades, the author had not understood at all what the "I AM" is or how to focus on it. It was a willingness to allow all the old views to be swept away, if necessary.

Ramana Maharshi had said Self-inquiry is more like feeling than like thought. Asking "Who am I?" or asking "To whom do these thoughts arise?" are easy instructions to follow as long as one stays in the realm of thought.

However, when it comes to feeling "Who am I?"
or feeling "I AM," the instructions had always been vague.
What exactly is the feeling I AM?
How do I know I AM?

Nisargadatta Maharaj and many others had said
the "I AM" is consciousness.
The author wondered: "is the 'I AM' the 'I thought'
or is the 'I AM' just my present awareness?"
The author thought: "if the 'I AM' is this present
awareness, the awareness that is now looking at this room,
then paying attention to the 'I AM' is just:
My awareness watching my awareness."

This was a revelation! Instead of having some vague
practice where one is told to pay attention to the "I AM"
without ever being sure exactly what the "I AM" is
and feels like, here was an absolutely clear instruction:
My present awareness watching my present awareness.

Not some unknown, seemingly far away awareness
labeled the Infinite Self or labeled God. This awareness,
my awareness, here and now watching itself,
while ignoring thought, the body, the world, etc.

Immediately the author tried this practice:
Turning the attention away from thought and towards
awareness watching awareness. The author shut his eyes,
because the point was also to ignore the world.
To turn the attention that normally goes out into the world
around 180 degrees and to look inward.
To turn the attention away from thoughts, feelings and
desires and towards awareness watching awareness.
If the author noticed a thought, he ignored the thought
and brought the attention back to
awareness watching awareness.
Awareness paying attention to awareness to the exclusion
of all else. Awareness paying attention only to itself.
46

The results were instant!
From the very first moment one tries this practice,
one is abiding as awareness!
There is no waiting! It is easy. This is not meant to imply
that from the beginning the ego ends. It takes years
of continuous practice before the ego meets its final end.
However, from the moment one tries this easy to
understand practice, one is being as awareness!

The author practiced the Awareness Watching
Awareness Method for two years, from December 2001
to January 2004. There were more days with twelve hours
of practice than days with two hours of practice.
In January of 2004 the author's ego, sorrow and suffering
came to its final end, and what remained is
Infinite-Eternal-Awareness-Love-Bliss.
Thus the Awareness Watching Awareness Method
once again lived up to its reputation as being
the most direct and rapid means to eternal bliss
in this lifetime.

Ramana Maharshi and Nisargadatta Maharaj
had both specifically described the Awareness Watching
Awareness Method; however, the author's ego
did not allow him to pay attention to those quotes.
The Awareness Watching Awareness Method was like
a buried treasure, hidden among so many other quotes
on so many different subjects.
In the Step Seven quotes in *The Seven Steps to Awakening*
you can read the way Nisargadatta Maharaj, Sadhu Om,
Ramana Maharshi, Sankara, Vasistha, Annamalai Swami
and Muruganar describe the awareness practice.

Another reason the author did not previously realize
the true meaning of I AM is that he had read that the
"I AM," the true Self, is infinite continuous awareness.

That made it seem like the "I AM" must be something different from the awareness that *appears* to wake up in the morning. However, the habit of always looking outward is what causes the awareness to *appear* to wake up in the morning and to *seem* limited.
The awareness does not really wake up in the morning and it is not limited.
Waking up, going to sleep and limitation are illusions created by the habit of always looking outward.
If one observes the awareness for many years, eventually one discovers that
the awareness is continuous and that it is not limited.

The significance of the Awareness Watching Awareness discovery is one of communication.
A human could be told to focus on the I AM and even after one hundred million imaginary lifetimes, still not know what the I AM is. (While telling themselves and believing that they do know in practice what the I AM is).
However, if told that the I AM is the awareness that *appears* to wake up in the morning, the background of awareness that is there during all the waking hours, and given specific instructions in how to turn the attention away from thought, etc., and towards awareness watching awareness, one can end the ego and suffering in this lifetime and remain eternally in bliss.
Those specific practice instructions are in Chapter Seven in the book you are now reading.

You might think that the majority of humans would rejoice at the discovery of the most direct and rapid means to eternal bliss. Due to the tricks of the ego, the majority of humans will not rejoice at the discovery. That is why this book begins by identifying the impostor, exposing its motivations and tricks, showing the importance of awakening the extremely intense desire for Freedom, and giving step-by-step instructions
for such an awakening.

Historically, not even one in a million humans has been dedicated to the direct experience of the eternal Truth that lives within them and is their true Self. The Awareness Watching Awareness Method is the most direct and rapid means for a human to end all sorrow and suffering and to remain in infinite-eternal-awareness-love-bliss.

The Awareness Watching Awareness Method is the most direct and rapid means for a person of the Jewish faith to directly experience the "I AM" that was revealed to Moses. The Awareness Watching Awareness Method is the most direct and rapid means for a Christian to discover and live in the Kingdom of Heaven within in direct experience in this lifetime. The Awareness Watching Awareness Method is the most direct and rapid means for a "Hindu" to attain Freedom while living (jivanmukti) and to live in Being-Awareness-Bliss (sat-chit-ananda). The Awareness Watching Awareness Method is the most direct and rapid means for a Muslim to know the true Self. The Prophet Mohammad said, "He who knows his Self knows his Lord." The Awareness Watching Awareness Method is the most direct and rapid means for a Buddhist to attain the bliss of Nirvana and to bring the ego, suffering, desire and craving to their final end.

The ego has distorted all of the religious and spiritual teachings of the past. The result is that all of the religious and spiritual teachings of the past now serve the ego and hide the most direct and rapid means to Freedom. What has happened with all of the religious and spiritual teachings of the past is that the ego in the reader or listener cooperates with the ego in the so-called "spiritual teacher" to produce a teaching that will serve the ego. Then both the "spiritual teacher" and the student call the false teaching "a true teaching."

The "spiritual teacher" has different names in different spiritual traditions. Some examples of this are: preacher, priest, minister, rabbi, master, guru, roshi, lama, imam, murshid, translator, etc. The spiritual and religious teachings of the past are lineages of egotism that are falsely labeled and promoted as lineages of truth.

Some of the spiritual teachings of the past were authentic spiritual teachings given by awakened sages. However, the moment an awakened sage speaks, the ego in the listener begins to distort the teachings. Therefore, the distortion does not take time to begin. The distortion begins immediately. Once the teaching has been distorted by the ego, the teaching serves the ego. The ego distortion becomes even greater as time passes. The ego distortion can always be seen in both the written and spoken words of the spiritual and religious teachings of the past. There will be many false ego teachings in the future also. Consider this quote by Lao Tzu from the Hua Hu Ching: *"Not all spiritual paths lead to the Harmonious Oneness. Indeed, **most** are detours and distractions, **nothing more**."*

It is possible to extract helpful quotes from the spiritual teachings of the past; however, the quotes must be extracted by an awakened sage. If an attempt to extract quotes is made by one in whom the ego illusion has not yet come to its final end, some or all of the quotes selected will serve the ego.

Because it is the most direct and rapid means to end human misery and to live eternally in Peace-joy, the Awareness Watching Awareness Method is of great benefit even to those who are not spiritually inclined.

50

What might seem like only a slight difference
in the way one practices makes a huge, profound,
extraordinary, quantum leap of a difference
in the speed of the results.
What might seem like only a slight difference in the way
one practices can save years or even lifetimes of practice.
Therefore, the precision with which
the practice instructions are described is crucial.
A slight change in the wording of the practice instructions
will produce a slight change in the practice,
thereby making the practice indirect,
thus losing the rapid results.
There are other methods that appear similar to the
Awareness Watching Awareness Method; however,
seemingly similar methods will not produce the same
rapid results and they will not save the years or lifetimes
of practice. Those other methods are different from the
Awareness Watching Awareness Method
and those differences destroy the efficiency.
In the Awareness Watching Awareness Method
no external teacher is needed.
All that is required in the
Awareness Watching Awareness Method
is that one has the precise practice instructions
and that one follows them by practicing.
At first the written instructions are the teacher;
then the practice is the teacher.
The written instructions are the teacher only for the time
it takes you to read them or listen to them,
if you decide to record them.
Therefore, the teacher is
the Awareness Watching Awareness practice.
The Awareness Watching Awareness practice
is the true, real, enduring teacher.
You never need to physically see a teacher
on this Direct Path.
Physically seeing a teacher would draw your attention
outward and would be counterproductive.

Instructions for practicing the
Awareness Watching Awareness Method
are in Chapter Seven.

Consider giving the Awareness Watching Awareness
practice a sincere, fair try.
A few months is not long enough to be a sincere, fair try.

The awakening of the
extremely intense desire for Freedom
will make the Awareness Watching Awareness practice
far more effective.

Self honesty will make the
Awareness Watching Awareness practice
far more effective.

Read Chapter Six very slowly three times
before reading Chapter Seven.

CHAPTER SEVEN

THE AWARENESS WATCHING AWARENESS METHOD

PRACTICE INSTRUCTIONS

PRELIMINARY INSTRUCTIONS:

Set aside as much time every day
to practice the Awareness Watching Awareness Method
as you are willing to set aside.
Every day drop as many unnecessary activities
as you can to create more time to practice
the Awareness Watching Awareness Method.
If you are not willing to drop all unnecessary activities,
in order to create the maximum amount of time every day
for practice, then you can read Chapter Five and Chapter
Thirteen in *The Direct Means to Eternal Bliss* and the Step
Five quotes in *The Seven Steps to Awakening* every day
until the extremely intense desire for Freedom awakens in
you. Eating food and taking a shower
are examples of necessary activities.
For some people working to earn a living
is an example of a necessary activity.
For some people taking care of their children
is an example of a necessary activity.
Some categories of **un**necessary activities are
entertainment, hobbies, etc.

Practice for at least two hours every day.
Use all of your free time for practice, and practice for the
maximum number of hours per day you are able to. If
you are retired and can practice for twelve hours every day,
consider doing so.
It is better if you can be undisturbed and alone
during your practice.

If you practice at home, you can ask the people you live with not to disturb you when you are practicing unless there is an emergency. Or you can find some other place to practice where you will not be disturbed.
A quiet place is best.

Bodily posture is not important in the Awareness Watching Awareness Method. However, since one wishes to turn the attention away from the body, it is important that the body is comfortable and relaxed and not causing any pain.
You can do the practice sitting crossed legged, or sitting on a chair, or sitting on a sofa or couch, or even lying down on your bed if you are able to do so without falling asleep. Make sure the posture is comfortable and does not cause any pain or strain. Make sure the posture helps you to ignore the body and turn your attention away from the body. Make sure the posture does not cause your attention to be directed towards the body.

For the purposes of this practice, the following definitions of the words *awareness* and *thought* must be used:

Thought: Thoughts are the words of your native language in your mind. If your native language is English, thoughts are those English words in your mind.
If you are fluent in two languages, then thoughts are the words of those two languages in your mind.

Awareness: When you wake up from sleep, awareness is that consciousness that woke up from sleep.
Thoughts come and thoughts go.
The background of awareness does not come and go.
The background of awareness is continuous during all your waking hours until you go to sleep again.
Awareness is you, your consciousness, just your awareness that is looking through your eyes right now.
54

The words awareness, consciousness, attention, observing, watching, looking, seeing and concentrating all have the same meaning in the practice instructions. Awareness is not thought. Awareness is that which is conscious of thought or conscious of the absence of thought. Both when there are thoughts and when there are no thoughts the background of awareness is aware. The background of awareness is continuous during all of the waking hours until you go to sleep again. During deep sleep, the thinker is no longer aware of the background of awareness. Awareness is not emotions. Awareness is that which is conscious of emotions or conscious of the absence of emotions. Both when there are emotions and when there are no emotions, the background of awareness is aware, because your awareness is continuous during all of the waking hours until you go to sleep again. Awareness is not the objects seen by the eyes. Awareness is that which is conscious of the objects seen by the eyes or conscious of the absence of the objects seen by the eyes. Your awareness is aware when the eyes are open seeing objects and when your eyes are closed not seeing objects, because your awareness is continuous during all the waking hours until you go to sleep again. Awareness is not the thought "I." Awareness is that which is conscious of the thought "I" or conscious of the absence of the thought "I." Both when you think "I" and when you do not think "I," your awareness is aware, because your awareness is continuous during all the waking hours. Awareness is not desire. Awareness is that which is conscious of desire or conscious of the absence of desire. Both when there is desire and when there is no desire, you are aware, because your awareness is continuous until you go to sleep again. Awareness is not something far away or mysterious. Awareness is that which is looking through your eyes reading this sentence. Just your ordinary, everyday awareness. Not some special awareness.

Awareness is that which wakes up in the morning
and remains conscious until you go to sleep at night.
Awareness is not any of the things or experiences
perceived. Awareness is that which is conscious
of the things or experiences. Awareness is also that
which is conscious of the absence of things or experiences.

The following practice instructions are the
Awareness Watching Awareness Method described
with carefully chosen slightly different words.
The practice instructions are called Descriptions.
Use only one Description per practice session.
If you are going to practice for one, two or three hours
today, then for that entire time,
you should use the same Description.
Try Description A first. Use a different Description each
day until you have tried all of the Descriptions.
Then choose the Description
that was the easiest for you to understand and to practice,
and from then on use only that Description.

Some Descriptions might for a moment have you
start with your eyes open, however, once you are
instructed to close your eyes, keep your eyes closed.
The Awareness Watching Awareness Method
is always practiced with the eyes closed.
When you are observing your awareness,
just remain with that.
There is no need to do anything else. Awareness is empty.
It is just awareness being aware of itself.
It is not a special type of awareness.
It is just your ordinary everyday awareness
that you normally go through the day with,
looking at itself.
You can make an audio recording of the Descriptions
on an audiocassette, CD or Mp3 etc., for your personal use.
Record only one Description per recording.
Listen to only one Description during a practice session.
56

It is better not to interrupt your practice session by having to turn your recording off. That is why it is best to record only one Description per recording.
Repeat the same Description on the recording every thirty minutes.

THE AWARENESS WATCHING AWARENESS METHOD

PRACTICE INSTRUCTIONS

Description A: Shut your eyes.
Notice your awareness. Observe your awareness.
Turn your attention away from the world, body and thought and towards awareness watching awareness.
Every time you notice you are thinking,
turn your attention away from thought
and back towards awareness watching awareness.
Watch your awareness, not your thoughts.

Description B: Look out at the room
and notice your awareness looking out through your eyes.
Now shut your eyes and notice the same awareness is still there that a moment ago was looking outward at the room.
Observe that awareness.
If you notice thoughts, ignore the thoughts
and turn your attention away from the thoughts
and towards awareness observing awareness.

Description C: Shut your eyes.
Notice that you are conscious. Watch that consciousness.
Every time you notice a thought,
turn your attention away from the thought
and continue watching your consciousness.
Do *not* watch your thoughts. Watch your consciousness.
Consciousness watching consciousness.
Consciousness conscious of consciousness.

Description D: Shut your eyes.
Turn your attention away from thought
and watch the watcher.

Description E: Shut your eyes.
Notice your awareness. Be aware of your awareness.
If you notice you are thinking, turn your attention
away from thought and towards awareness of awareness.

Description F: Shut your eyes.
Just remain in awareness aware of itself. If there are
thoughts, turn your attention away from the thoughts
and back to awareness aware of itself.

Description G: Shut your eyes.
You observe your awareness.
Whenever there are thoughts,
turn your observation away from the thoughts
and continue to observe your awareness.

Description H: Shut your eyes. Turn your attention
towards awareness and concentrate on awareness.
Concentrate in a relaxed manner without effort.
Every time thoughts are noticed,
turn your attention away from the thoughts
and back towards concentrating on awareness.

Description I: Shut your eyes. Be aware of being
aware. Now remain in that awareness of awareness.
If there are thoughts, turn your awareness away from
the thoughts and continue being aware of being aware.

Description J: Shut your eyes.
Notice you are aware. Look at that awareness.
Remain in awareness looking at awareness.
If thoughts arise, look away from the thoughts
and continue looking at awareness.
Remain in that awareness looking at awareness.
58

Description K: Shut your eyes.
Your present awareness watching your present awareness,
while ignoring all else.

Description L: Look at the room.
Notice your attention looking through your eyes. Shut
your eyes and turn your attention around to look at itself.
Attention attending to attention. Remain with that.
Don't move from that. Don't attend to anything else.
Don't attend to thought. Attend only to attention.

Description M: Look at the room. Notice your
awareness looking through your eyes. Now shut your eyes.
Notice that same awareness that was looking through your
eyes a moment ago. Now turn that awareness around 180
degrees away from the world, the body and thought and
towards itself, towards awareness aware of awareness.

Description N: Look at the room, or if you are
outdoors look at the sky. Your awareness is the seer.
Shut your eyes. See the seer.
Turn your attention away from thought
and towards the seer.

Description O: Shut your eyes.
Turn your attention away from the known.
Now know the knower.

Description P: Shut your eyes.
Awareness aware only of awareness.
Remain there. Dwell there. Be there. Live there.

Description Q: Shut your eyes.
One awareness observing one awareness.
Not two, one observing the other. Only one.
Observe your awareness. If you notice thinking,
do not attempt to complete the thought. Drop the thought,
let go of the thought as though you had no interest
in the thought. Continue observing your awareness.

Description R: Shut your eyes.
Observe your awareness. Relax into your awareness.
Remain there in awareness aware only of awareness.

Description S: Shut your eyes.
Turn your awareness away from
what your awareness is aware of
and towards awareness aware only of itself.

Description T: Shut your eyes.
Directly experience awareness by observing awareness
and relaxing into awareness.
Rest in awareness of awareness.
Rest in awareness aware only of itself.
Remain in awareness.
Do not remain in thought.

Description U: There are the things you are aware
of. There is the awareness that is aware of the things.
Instead of observing the things, observe the awareness.
Shut your eyes. There are thoughts and feelings.
There is the awareness that is aware
of the thoughts and feelings.
Instead of observing the thoughts and feelings,
observe the awareness.

Description V: Shut your eyes.
Do not observe thought. Observe awareness.
Awareness observing awareness is empty.
There is no thing to observe there. Don't complicate it
by thinking there is more to it. Awareness is subtle.
In awareness observing awareness there is only awareness.
It is simple. Remain in awareness observing itself.

Description W: Shut your eyes.
Focus on the awareness that thoughts are arising in.
Do *not* focus on the thoughts. Thoughts come and
thoughts go. The awareness in which thoughts are arising
does not come and go.
Be aware of the awareness that does not come and go.
When there are thoughts, watch the awareness,
not the thoughts.
When there are no thoughts, watch the awareness.
Thoughts or no thoughts,
continue to observe the awareness.
Continue to relax in and be aware of awareness.
Remain there. Dwell there. Be there. Live there.

Description X: Shut your eyes.
If you see darkness, turn your attention away from the
darkness and towards awareness of awareness.
If you see light, turn your attention away from the light
and towards awareness aware only of awareness.
If you notice your breathing,
turn your attention away from the breathing
and towards awareness aware only of awareness.
Whatever you become aware of,
turn your attention away from it
and towards awareness of awareness.

Description Y: Shut your eyes.
Awareness *not* aware of thoughts.
Awareness *not* aware of emotions.
Awareness *not* aware of anything except awareness.
Awareness aware of nothing except awareness.
The background of awareness
aware only of the background of awareness.
Awareness aware only of awareness.
Awareness only.
Awareness alone.

Description Z: Shut your eyes.
Let go of the idea that you own awareness.
Let go of the idea that you control awareness.
Let the infinite awareness be what it is
without your trying to control it.
Relax and observe the awareness.
Let go of everything and observe the awareness.
Relax completely and observe the awareness.
With as little effort as possible
and with a gentle, kind, easy, relaxed, loving approach;
observe the awareness.

Read Chapter Seven very slowly three times
before reading Chapter Eight.

CHAPTER EIGHT

FURTHER CLARIFICATION OF THE

AWARENESS WATCHING AWARENESS METHOD

These further clarifications have been placed in a separate chapter because the practice instructions for the Awareness Watching Awareness Method are simple and they should remain simple. It is not helpful to bring concepts with you into the practice. It is best just to focus on the simple practice instructions.

One of the things you might wonder about is what to do after you start watching your awareness. There is nothing else to be done. You just continue with awareness watching awareness. There are no objects to see. Awareness is empty. There is no thing to observe in awareness. Just continue for the entire practice session watching your awareness. Only awareness watching awareness and nothing else. The key is to be content just watching your awareness and not to move from that and not to add anything to that. Just be content with awareness watching awareness. You should look at it like awareness watching awareness is all there is, there is nothing more.

The best practice session is when there are no thoughts. If there are thoughts, turn your attention away from the thoughts and towards awareness watching awareness. Do not encourage thoughts. Do not try to complete a thought. Do not turn your attention towards thoughts. Do not think about thinking. If thoughts are happening, do not make a problem out of it. Just turn your attention away from thoughts and towards awareness watching awareness. Just remain with awareness watching awareness.

When awareness is watching awareness
something extraordinary is happening.
You are for the first time turning inward.
Your true nature is awareness.
What you really are at your core is awareness.
Therefore, in awareness watching awareness,
you are for the first time observing and knowing yourself.
The reason for pointing out that you are doing something
extraordinary while practicing awareness watching
awareness is because at first you might think, "what else?"
or "so what?" Just continue to practice and forget about
"what else?" or "so what?" By turning your attention away
from thought and towards awareness watching awareness,
you are doing something that will change your life
completely, if you are sincere and continue to practice.
Most humans live their entire lives always looking outward
at people, places and things.
By turning your attention away from the world, body
and thought and towards awareness watching awareness,
you are doing something extraordinary.

It might take a few days, a few weeks, or for some
people a few months to start to feel something.
At first it is subtle and you won't know what it is.
You will know that you like it. It is pleasant.
A new subtle feeling.
You are beginning to feel eternal-life-love-peace.

While you are practicing
the Awareness Watching Awareness Method:
Just stay there. Relax there. Don't seek something other
than awareness watching awareness. Don't seek any other
state. Just remain in awareness watching awareness.
Be happy that it is simple. Don't seek more than that.
It is just a simple state. Just remain with awareness
watching awareness, and every time a thought arises
turn your awareness away from the thought
and towards awareness watching awareness.
64

Continue to practice every day. Look at it as though all you were seeking was the awareness watching awareness itself and not something else. Be content with staying in awareness watching awareness without moving from it. Some days the mind may be noisy, however, if you keep on practicing, a good day will appear when your practice will go very deep without your trying to make it go deep. Just be content to remain with awareness watching awareness, regardless if it seems like a good practice session or not. Some days your emotions may be turbulent. Ignore the turbulent feelings and turn your attention away from the emotions and towards awareness watching awareness.

If you continue practicing the Awareness Watching Awareness Method every day, eventually you will start to enjoy awareness watching awareness. How long it will take to begin enjoying awareness watching awareness is different for different people. It may take days, weeks or for some people months before they begin to enjoy the practice. The point is, if you find it difficult to remain with awareness watching awareness in the beginning, don't give up. Practice every day on the good days and on the noisy-mind or turbulent-feeling days also. Just continue turning your attention away from thoughts and towards awareness watching awareness.

The best kind of awareness watching awareness practice session is one that is empty. Awareness watching awareness and nothing else. Just stay there. Just be there. Dwell there. Remain there. Don't seek anything different; just be content with awareness watching awareness. *Relax* and continue watching your awareness.

Here is a way to look at it:
Awareness watching awareness is similar to falling in love. You spend time with someone. You watch them. You observe them. You do not yet know them.

You continue to observe them. You don't have
expectations, because you don't know them well enough
yet to have expectations. You continue to observe them.
Some days you have pleasant feelings while you observe
them. Some days you have unpleasant feelings
while you observe them. You continue to observe them.
Every day you come to know them better, even though
you may not be aware that you are coming to know them
better. Then one day, suddenly and unexpectedly, you fall
in Love. Awareness watching awareness is similar to that.
Just don't expect anything, and continue watching your
awareness. The fact that nothing is happening is great!
If it seems like day after day it is just the same,
only awareness watching awareness; that is great!
Just remain content with that.
Look at awareness watching awareness as enough,
just as it is. Continue your practice every day.
When will you fall in love with awareness watching
awareness? It may be after one month or after many
months of practice. There is plenty of confirmation along
the way. Do not be concerned about whether you are
progressing or not. Progress may be imperceptible to the
practitioner. Some people will reach the point where just
closing their eyes brings awareness-joy
even before they have started the practice.
Some people may experience turbulence
for many years before peace or vice versa.
Persevere and continue to practice.

You can look upon your awareness as something
that wants you to watch it without expecting anything from
it, like someone who wants to be loved for what they are
and not for what they can give you.
What you truly are is
Infinite-Eternal-Awareness-Love-Bliss.
By having your attention turned towards the world, body
and thought all the time, you imagine you are a body
subject to disease, death and suffering.

By turning your attention towards awareness,
you are for the first time observing what you are.
Don't watch your thoughts. Turn your attention away
from your thoughts and watch your empty awareness.
Observe the observing. Observe the awareness.

If you remain content with awareness watching
awareness, your problems will start to disappear.
Your misery will start to disappear.
Peace will come unexpectedly.
Joy will come unexpectedly.
Infinite Love will come unexpectedly.

Awareness watching awareness is awareness being
awareness. Because of the long ancient habit of looking
outward towards people, places and things, the word
"watching" is used in *some* of the practice instructions.
One takes that same habit of watching people, places and
things and shuts the eyes and turns it inwards towards
awareness watching awareness. That is why the word
"watching" is used in *some* of the practice instructions.

What is real is awareness watching awareness,
looking inward. What is unreal is looking outward
towards the world of people, places and things.
Looking outward brings suffering, death and futility.

Watching thoughts is *not* looking inward.
Watching feelings is *not* looking inward.
Watching breathing is *not* looking inward.
Only turning the attention away from the observed
and towards the observer is looking inward.
Only awareness watching awareness is looking inward.

Looking inward is eternal Freedom.
Looking inward is eternal life.
Looking inward is eternal awareness.
Looking inward is eternal peace.
Looking inward is eternal joy.
Looking inward is eternal Love that is absolutely perfect
and free of all forms of sorrow and misery.

That joy, that perfection, is your awareness.
Because you always looked outward, you never
experienced it. To change the long habit
of looking outward, you need to practice every day.
Practice for as many hours every day as you can.
If you only practice the Awareness Watching Awareness
Method for thirty minutes per day and spend the other
twenty-three and a half hours looking outward,
you will not progress very quickly. If you want rapid
results, drop all your unnecessary activities to create the
maximum amount of time to practice for many hours
every day. Maybe once per week, you can devote the whole
day to practicing awareness watching awareness.
To come to know, experience, and live in
Infinite-Eternal-Awareness-Love-Bliss
is definitely worth the time spent practicing.

You'll discover you're not a body living in a world.
You are eternal awareness, perfect love-joy.

If it seems boring the first few times you try
the awareness watching awareness practice that is okay.
Continue to practice.

Read Chapter Eight very slowly three times
before reading Chapter Nine.

CHAPTER NINE

THE ABANDON RELEASE METHOD

If your ego will not allow you to practice the
Awareness Watching Awareness Method,
the Abandon Release Method is the next best choice.
The Awareness Watching Awareness Method
is more effective than the Abandon Release Method.
Therefore, if your ego will allow you to practice it,
the Awareness Watching Awareness Method should be
your first choice. If one looks at the thousands of spiritual
practices that have been taught to humans in the past,
the Awareness Watching Awareness Method is the most
direct and rapid means to bring suffering and the ego
to their final end in this lifetime.
The Awareness Watching Awareness Method
is the most direct and rapid means to living in
infinite-eternal-awareness-love-bliss in this lifetime.
If one looks at the thousands of spiritual practices that
have been taught to humans in the past, the Abandon
Release Method is the second most rapid means to bring
suffering and the ego to their final end in this lifetime.
If one looks at the thousands of spiritual practices that
have been taught to humans in the past, the Abandon
Release Method is the second most rapid means to living
in infinite-eternal-awareness-love-bliss in this lifetime.

The Abandon Release Method is easier to practice
than the Awareness Watching Awareness Method,
even when you are tired or sleepy.
If your ego will not allow you to practice
the Awareness Watching Awareness Method,
you could practice the Abandon Release Method for one
year. Then you could switch to the Awareness Watching
Awareness Method and practice it exclusively.

Or you could continue practicing the
Abandon Release Method for as many years as you wish.
You should practice one of the primary methods:
the Awareness Watching Awareness Method
or the Abandon Release Method, or the
Loving Consciousness Method for the rest of your life.

The reason practice should continue for as long as
the body lives is: There is a false state of Freedom,
where the ego has not come to its final end, and has only
been temporarily submerged in the infinite awareness.
This temporary state is very similar to eternal Freedom,
there is no suffering and one only has the experience of
infinite-awareness-love-bliss.
One in this temporary state will usually
have the perception that they have been liberated.
However, one in this temporary state has not been
liberated. The ego will sooner or later reappear.
In True Freedom, the ego never reappears. In True
Freedom, the ego is gone forever. That is the reason
one should practice for as long as the body lives,
even if one has the perception that one has been liberated.

The preliminary instructions for the
Abandon Release Method are the same as for the
Awareness Watching Awareness Method.
See Chapter Seven for the preliminary instructions.
In the beginning, the best position for the practice of the
Abandon Release Method is lying down on your bed.
After you have practiced the Abandon Release Method
many times while lying down, then you could try the
practice sitting up. After you have practiced the Abandon
Release Method many times in both positions,
sitting up and lying down,
you can choose the position you like best
and then continue to practice in that position.

The following is a suggested schedule
for using the Abandon Release Method Descriptions:
Start by using the Description D practice instructions
for the first month.
In other words, use Description D for thirty days.
Use Description E for the second month.
Continue using Description E for thirty days.
Use Description A for the third month.
Continue using Description A for thirty days.
Use Description B for the fourth month.
Continue using Description B for thirty days.
Use Description A (again) for the fifth month.
Continue using Description A for thirty days.
Begin using Description C.
Continue to use Description C for one to four years.

Once per month, as a reminder,
for one practice session, use Description A.
In other words, use Description C every day,
and one day per month switch to Description A.
After one to four years of practice you may be
so familiar with the practice, Description F is all you need.
If after one to four years of practice you switch to
Description F, once per month for one practice session
you should use Description C,
and once per year for one practice session
you should use Description A.

Like any skill,
the more you practice, the more skill you gain.
The longer you practice,
the more enjoyable the practice becomes,
after you have gained some skill in letting go.
Some people will enjoy the Abandon Release Method
from the beginning.
Other people will find the practice easy and enjoyable
after many weeks of practicing every day.

You can make a recording of the practice
instructions (Descriptions A, B, C, D, E or F) on an audio
cassette, CD, or Mp3 etc., for your personal use,
and then play it during your practice session,
repeating the instructions on the recording
every thirty minutes.
Pause for one minute between each sentence
when making the recording.
Put a "do not disturb" sign on your bedroom door,
turn off the lights, and lie down on your bed.
If lying down flat on your back becomes tiresome
you can change positions by turning over on your side.

THE ABANDON RELEASE METHOD

PRACTICE INSTRUCTIONS

Description A: Shut your eyes. Relax your body.
Now ignore your body. Let go of all effort. Let go of all
sense of having to do something, as though there is
nothing you have to do and nothing you have to think
about. Letting go of all effort means letting go of all will
and all desire, as though there is nothing that needs to be
accomplished or changed. Let go. Relax. Let go more.
Relax more. See how far it is possible to let go.
Let go of all thoughts. Let go of all feelings.
Let go of all effort.
Let go of everything except your awareness.
Whatever thoughts, perceptions, images or feelings arise
let them go as soon as they arise or even before they arise.
Do not follow thoughts, as though you had no interest in
thoughts. Let go of all your perceptions
as if your perceptions have nothing to do with you.
Continue to relax more and more.
Throughout the practice session let go more, then let go
even more and as the practice session continues, see how
far it is possible to let go. Relax completely. Let go totally.
72

Release everything except your awareness. Letting go is giving up completely. Letting go is surrendering completely. Letting go is relaxing completely. Letting go is releasing completely.
Letting go is letting go of all effort and all thought. Letting go is letting go of all feelings, desires and images. Letting go is letting go of everything except your awareness. The difference between falling asleep and the Abandon Release Method is that when you fall asleep you let go of everything including your awareness. In the Abandon Release Method you let go of everything except your awareness.

Description B: Shut your eyes. Relax your body. Release your body. Relax all effort. Release all effort. Relax all your thoughts. Release all your thoughts. Continue throughout the practice session to see how much you can relax and release your thoughts, feelings and desires. Relax and release everything except your awareness. Relax totally. Relax completely. Release totally. Release completely.

Description C: Shut your eyes.
Let go of all effort.
Let go of all thought.
Let go of everything except your awareness.
Whatever arises let it go.
Relax, release, let go.
Continue to relax, release and let go completely.
See how far it is possible to let go of all effort and all thought. See how far it is possible to let go of everything except your awareness.

Description D: Shut your eyes.
Let go of all effort. Continue to let go of all effort
during the entire practice session.
Let go of effort more and more
and see how far it is possible to let go of effort.
Relax and continue to relax.
Relax more and more throughout the entire
practice session. Totally let go of all effort.

Description E: Shut your eyes.
Let go of all thoughts.
If a thought arises, let it go.
If another thought arises, let it go.
Continue to let go of thought. Relax thought completely.
Continue to release thought throughout the practice
session. See how far it is possible to let go of thought.
Do not try to complete a thought, let the thought go
immediately when the thought first begins.
Let go completely.

Description F: Shut your eyes.
Let go completely.
Totally let go.
Let go of everything except your awareness.

Read Chapter Nine very slowly three times
before reading Chapter Ten.

CHAPTER TEN

THE ETERNAL METHOD

The purpose of the Eternal Method is to provide
a sense of the limitless nature of eternal life
and to focus the attention on the eternal.
Any position is okay for this practice.
Lying down on your bed with the lights turned off is the
best position. You may record the instructions for your
personal use. Pause for one minute between each sentence
when making the recording.
The Eternal Method is a secondary practice,
not a primary practice; therefore, the Eternal Method
should not be practiced more often than once per week.

THE ETERNAL METHOD PRACTICE INSTRUCTIONS

Shut your eyes.
Imagine you are traveling back in time.
Go back in time one hundred billion years.
Go back in time one hundred billion more years.
You are now so far back in time the earth does not exist.
Imagine you are traveling back in time one trillion years
further into the past. Go back in time one trillion more
years. Imagine you are traveling back in time
eight hundred trillion years further into the past.
Now travel back eight hundred trillion years
further into the past.
Imagine that you are traveling at the rate of eight hundred
trillion years per second into the past and that you have
now traveled for one hundred trillion years at that rate.

The contents of what was called the universe
at the time you lived on earth, do not yet exist at this time.
None of the stars or planets that existed
at the time you lived on earth exists yet,
because you are now in a time before they existed.

Travel eight hundred trillion years further back in time.
Realize now that no matter how long you continue to travel
back in time, you will not come any closer to
the eternal past, because the eternal past goes on forever.

Now travel another eight hundred trillion years
further into the past. Now imagine you have traveled
another eight hundred trillion years further into the past.
Now travel another eight hundred trillion years
further into the past.

Realize that no matter how long you continue to
travel into the past, even if you travel at the rate of eight
hundred trillion years per second for a hundred trillion
years, you will not come closer to the eternal past,
because the eternal past always was, forever.

Look into the eternal past and see: *always was.*
The objects in space come and go;
however, the space is eternal.
Realize the meaning of the eternal past.
See: the eternal past goes on forever and ever.
Look into the eternal past, which goes on forever and ever,
and see the meaning of *always was.*
Look into the eternal past and see
the eternal past has no beginning.
Look into the eternal past and see the meaning of *no end.*
Realize: the eternal past has no end.
Look into the eternal past and see:
the eternal past goes on forever and never ends.

Now come back to the present time.
Imagine you are traveling forward in time.
Travel one hundred billion years into the future.
Now travel one hundred billion years further into the
future. You are now so far into the future
the earth and sun no longer exist.
Travel one trillion years further into the future.

Now imagine that you have traveled one trillion more years into the future. Now travel eight hundred trillion years further into the future.
Now imagine that you have traveled another eight hundred trillion years further into the future.
Imagine that you are traveling at the rate of eight hundred trillion years per second into the future and that you have traveled for one hundred trillion years at that rate.

You are now in a time when everything that existed during the time when you lived on earth, no longer exists. All of the stars and planets that existed at the time when you lived on earth, no longer exist. All of the things that you thought were so important when you lived on earth, have no importance now. Look at how all of the problems you thought you had when living on earth, have no significance now.

Look at how all those problems you had when you lived on earth did not have any real significance. You only imagined those problems had significance. What has real value and significance is the eternal. The eternal infinite space-awareness, which is eternal life, is what you are and what you always have been, and that is where all real significance, Truth, meaning, perfect safety, love and bliss are.

Now imagine you have traveled another eight hundred trillion years further into the future. Now travel another eight hundred trillion years into the future. Realize now that no matter how long you continue to travel into the future, you will not come any closer to the eternal future, because the eternal future goes on forever.

Now travel another eight hundred trillion years further into the future.

Now imagine you have traveled another
eight hundred trillion years further into the future.
Realize, no matter how long you continue to travel into
the future, even if you travel at the rate of eight hundred
trillion years per second for one hundred trillion years,
you will not come closer to the eternal future,
because the eternal future continues forever.

Now look into the eternal future
and see the meaning of *always will be.*
The objects in space come and go;
however, the space is eternal.
Realize the meaning of the eternal future.
See that the eternal future goes on and on forever.
See the eternal future that goes on forever and ever
and realize the meaning of always will be.
Look into the eternal future
and see the meaning of *no end.*
See: the eternal future has no end.
See the eternal future and see the meaning of
the eternal future goes on forever and never ends.

You are that eternal infinite space-awareness
that never ends. See the beauty of eternal life.

Come back to the present time
and dedicate every moment of your life to the realization
of the Direct Experience of who you really are at your core.
In your daily life don't let the impostor;
who is the mistaken identity called ego,
take you through distractions, detours
and activities that lead to the temporary,
because the temporary is meaningless, futile,
and leads to suffering.
Drop all distractions, detours, entertainment
and other useless activities
to create the maximum amount of time for the practice
of the most direct and rapid means to eternal bliss.

Never waste time. Never waste even one second.

Discover your Eternal Life in Direct Experience.
See who you really are at the core of your being.
See who you are at the core of your awareness.
The core of your awareness is infinite and eternal.

A wave on an ocean of consciousness
imagines there is a line separating it from the ocean.
One day the wave challenges that assumption
by diving deep down.
The wave discovers there is no line
separating it from the ocean.
The wave discovers there are no waves;
there is only the ocean.

You are infinite-eternal-awareness-love-bliss.
Realize who you are in Direct Experience.
Bring the impostor self to a final end.
Discover your true Self in Direct Experience.

Read Chapter Ten very slowly three times
before reading Chapter Eleven.

CHAPTER ELEVEN

THE INFINITE SPACE METHOD

When people practice the Awareness Watching Awareness Method, they often tend to have the perception that awareness is located in their head. Your awareness is not in your head. Your awareness is infinite. The Infinite Space Method helps to remove the perception that awareness is something in your head.
The Infinite Space Method
helps to provide a sense of the limitless nature of space. The Infinite Space Method is a secondary, not a primary method; therefore, the Infinite Space Method
should not be practiced more often than once per week.

You can practice the Infinite Space Method in any position; however, for the first time, try practicing lying down on your bed with the lights turned off.
You may record the instructions for your personal use. Pause for one minute between each sentence
when making the recording.

THE INFINITE SPACE METHOD

PRACTICE INSTRUCTIONS

Shut your eyes.
Imagine you are traveling into outer space,
in one direction, in a straight line.
Imagine you have traveled eight hundred trillion miles into outer space.
Continue in the same direction, along the same line, and travel another eight hundred trillion miles further into outer space.

Now imagine you have traveled another
eight hundred trillion miles further into space.
Now imagine you have traveled another
eight hundred trillion miles further in the same direction.

Now imagine that you are traveling at the speed of
one hundred thousand miles per second, and that you have
traveled for eight hundred trillion years at that speed,
in the same direction, along the same line.
Now travel for another eight hundred trillion years,
in the same direction,
at the rate of one hundred thousand miles per second.
No matter how fast you travel, and no matter how long
you travel, you have not come any closer to infinite space,
because infinite space never ends.

Now travel another eight hundred trillion miles,
in the same direction, along the same line.
Now imagine you have traveled
another eight hundred trillion miles in the same direction.
Now travel another eight hundred trillion miles
in the same direction, along the same line.

Now look forward in the same direction and see:
infinite space never ends.
Now look forward in the same direction and see:
space never ends.

Now travel another eight hundred trillion miles
further in the same direction, along the same line.
Now imagine you have traveled another
eight hundred trillion miles further in the same direction.

Now look forward in the same direction and see:
space goes on forever and ever.
See that even if you travel in the same direction for all
eternity, you will never come to the end,
because space never ends.

Look in the same direction and see infinite space.
Look in the same direction and see:
space goes on forever and there is no end.
Realize: space is never ending in all directions.

That infinite space is your awareness.
That infinite space is infinite love.
That infinite space is eternal life.

See the infinite Freedom of infinite space.
See: infinite space is open to allow everything.
Whatever wall or boundary you imagine;
there is infinite space on the other side of that boundary.
If you imagine a circle, there is always a larger circle,
and there is always infinite space
on the outside of the circle.

Now come back to earth.
Imagine you are sitting outdoors on a chair.
There is space in the atoms of your body.
There is space between the atoms of your body.
There is space in the molecules of your body.
Space is between the molecules of your body.
There is space in the cells of your body.
There is space between the cells of your body.
Your body is space.

Space in and between the atoms, molecules
and cells of your body
is touching the space in the atmosphere.
Space in the atmosphere is touching outer space.
The imagined boundaries are also space.
The earth, and everything on the earth, is space.
All the planets and stars in the universe are space.

There is only one space.
Space is the source of life.
Space is alive.

One infinite space.
One infinite Love.
You are that infinite Love.
One eternal-infinite-space-awareness-love-bliss.
You are that one
eternal-infinite-space-awareness-love-bliss.
There is only that one
eternal-infinite-space-awareness-love-bliss.

All the boundaries are imagined.
There are no real boundaries.
In Reality there is only the infinite Freedom
of infinite space.

From time to time in your daily life,
focus on the space, instead of on the objects.
Space inside the objects, space outside the objects,
and space in the imagined boundary.
Never again imagine that space is just nothing.
Space is that which is truly valuable.
Space is eternal life-awareness.
Space is infinite Love.
One being, one space, one infinite Love.

Focusing attention on space
is focusing attention on infinite Freedom.
Focusing attention on space
is focusing attention on infinite Love.
Your awareness is space.

All limits are imagined.
All limits are a product of delusion.
All limits are a type of dream.
It is possible to wake up.
You can wake up to the Reality of
infinite-eternal-space-awareness-love-bliss.
You can wake up to perfect peace.

You can wake up and discover
you have always been eternal-life-love-awareness-joy.
You can wake up and discover
you will always be eternal-life-love-awareness-joy.

Because of the long habit
of imagining you are a thinker living in a body in a world,
waking up requires spending much time
in the direct spiritual practice.
You are not a thinker living in a body in a world.
You are infinite-eternal-space-awareness-love-joy.

Read Chapter Eleven very slowly three times
before reading Chapter Twelve.

CHAPTER TWELVE

THE LOVING ALL METHOD

All of the methods that have been described in previous chapters are to be practiced when one is not engaged in any other activities. The question may arise, "What is the most effective method that can be practiced while one is engaged in other activities?"
The Loving All Method is the most effective method that can be practiced while one is engaged in other activities. The Loving All Method can be practiced everyday, during any and all types of activities.

PRACTICE INSTRUCTIONS

FOR THE LOVING ALL METHOD

The Loving All Method can be summed up as follows: *Love everything you perceive, exactly as it is. Love everything you experience, exactly the way it is.*

Love every thought you have, exactly as it is.
Love those thoughts you think are good,
exactly the way they are.
Love those thoughts you think are bad,
exactly the way they are.
Love all your emotions, exactly the way they are.
If you feel happy, love your happiness, exactly the way it is.
If you feel sad, love your sadness, exactly the way it is.
If you feel courage, love your courage, exactly the way it is.
If you feel fear, love your fear, exactly as it is.
If you feel love, love your feeling of love,
exactly the way it is.

If you feel anger, love your feeling of anger,
exactly the way it is.

Love your body, exactly the way it is.
Love the objects you see, exactly as they are.
Love the people you see, just the way they are.
Love your actions, just as they are.

Love everything you feel, think, say or do,
exactly the way it is.
Love everything you see, taste, touch, smell or hear,
exactly the way it is.
Love everything other people do, feel, think or say,
exactly the way it is.

If someone says something nice to you,
love what the person says, exactly the way it is.
If someone says something mean to you,
love what the person says, exactly the way it is.
If someone says to you,
"You are the nicest person I have ever met,"
love what the person said, exactly the way they said it.
If someone says to you,
"You are the most disgusting person I have ever met,"
love what the person said, exactly the way they said it.
If something nice happens during your day,
love it exactly the way it is.
If something horrible happens during your day,
love it exactly the way it is.

Love everything that happens, just the way it is.
Love every activity, exactly the way it is.
Love every experience, exactly the way it is.
Love everything, exactly the way it is.
Practice the Loving All Method during all your waking
hours. From the time you wake up in the morning
until the time you go to sleep at night,
practice the Loving All Method.
86

FURTHER CLARIFICATION

OF THE LOVING ALL METHOD

If you don't understand how to practice
using the word "love,"
you can substitute the words "emotionally allow"
for the word "love" in the practice instructions.
After practicing every day for one month
using the words "emotionally allow,"
you can substitute the words "emotionally accept"
for the word "love" in the practice instructions.

After practicing every day for one month
using the words "emotionally accept,"
you can go back to the original wording of the instructions,
just as they are, using the word "love,"
and then continue using the word "love" from then on.

The Loving All Method refers only to emotions.
No changes in external behavior are required.
For example, if a vase falls and you would normally try
and catch it, you will also try and catch the vase while
practicing the Loving All Method. You do not allow the
vase to fall because you love the falling.
You can love the falling and you can also love
the attempt at catching the vase. If someone were to try
to punch you in the face and you would normally duck,
you will also duck while practicing the Loving All Method.
Loving the fact that someone is trying to punch you
does not mean you will not duck.
You also love ducking to avoid being punched.

The Loving All Method is emotional acceptance.
The Loving All Method is not changing actions.
The Loving All Method is like any skill:
the more you practice, the more skill you gain.

If someone says something mean to you
and you feel bad emotionally because of what they said;
love the negative emotion as it is, and love yourself.
In the beginning, even though you are attempting to love
everything and every experience exactly as it is,
you may or may not succeed
in loving everything and every experience exactly as it is.
Changing the long time habit of emotionally rejecting
experiences will require much practice.

Love as much as you can love.
Continue to practice every day, trying to love everything
and every experience exactly the way it is.
After you have practiced for a few months,
you will gain more success at loving more experiences
exactly the way they are.
For some people, it may take years of practice
to be able to love all experiences.
However, great benefits come right from the beginning,
from the very first time you love an experience
that you would have previously rejected.
There is more love and energy in your life;
and life is lighter and easier. Therefore,
it is not as though you have to wait for some big payoff
at the end of the Loving All Method.
Each day you gain more skill at loving your experiences,
you have more love and energy on that very day.

Every day, try to love everything
and every experience that happens exactly the way it is.
The key word is *try*. Try means do it. You will learn how
by trying. You will learn how by doing it.
It might take some time to gain skill.
It might take some time to succeed. Some people
may have great success from the very first time they try.
Other people may have to practice for a few months
to see great changes in the ability to love
what previously seemed unlovable.

Loving everything the way it is includes emotional acceptance. Emotional acceptance does not prevent you from trying to change whatever you wish to change. What you wish to change, you will still change. Whatever action you would normally take to change something, you will take that same action while practicing the Loving All Method.

If you have a negative emotion while practicing the Loving All Method, you love the negative emotion. That may or may not change the negative emotion. Even if loving the negative emotion does not change the negative emotion, continue to love the negative emotion and the experiences that created the negative emotion exactly the way they are. Every day, continue to gain skill at loving negative emotions exactly as they are and eventually you may start to see some of the negative emotions change into love.

You should not look inward while engaged in daily activities. You should look outward while engaged in daily activities. In other words, it is important to pay attention to what you are doing while engaged in daily activities. The Loving All Method is not looking inward. It is important to pay close attention during your daily activities to minimize errors and problems. If you try to look inward during your daily activities, your activities may not flow smoothly. For example, if you try to look inward while putting toothpaste on your toothbrush, you might put shampoo or shaving cream on your toothbrush because your attention is divided between outward and inward.

The Loving All Method does not require much thought either. In the beginning you might need to think something like "Love every experience" many times every day while you are learning the practice.

However, after much practice you will not need that thinking reminder. The Loving All Method is a new feeling habit. The practice is feeling, not thinking.
Because the practice requires little or no thought
and is not a looking-inward method,
it can be practiced during all daily activities.

The Loving All Method is a way to develop
the habit of feeling love towards everything you perceive.
In the beginning you could try practicing
"no emotional resistance" during all of your daily
activities. In action you can resist all you want to resist.
If you would normally resist something in action,
you will continue to resist it in action while practicing the
Loving All Method. Not resisting emotionally
has nothing to do with what you do in your actions,
activities and behavior.
You can continue to resist all you wish to resist
in your actions, activities and behavior
while practicing the Loving All Method.
While you may be resisting in action, you do not resist
emotionally while practicing the Loving All Method.

Loving every experience exactly the way it is,
makes living much easier.
Loving every experience exactly the way it is,
frees energy that used to be wasted.
Loving every experience exactly the way it is,
can change your daily living to a life of radiant love.
Thus, the Loving All Method
can fill your life with energy, ease, love, and joy.
Love is far more than just emotional acceptance.
From time to time throughout the day think of the person
you love the most. Get in touch with the love that you feel
for them. Then use that same feeling of love
when practicing the Loving All Method.
Read Chapter Twelve very slowly three times
before reading Chapter Thirteen.

CHAPTER THIRTEEN

THE REMINDERS

Read Chapter Five and Chapter Thirteen every day
until the extremely intense desire for Freedom awakens.
You will know the extremely intense desire for Freedom
has awakened when you have dropped all unnecessary
activities to create the maximum amount of time
for spiritual practice.
If you do not do your spiritual practice every day,
eventually your life will become full of suffering.
If you do not do your spiritual practice every day,
eventually, sooner or later, you will experience
one or more of the thousands of
different types of suffering.
If you do not do your spiritual practice every day,
you will continue to be caught in the cycle of birth and
death, birth again, death again, birth again, death again,
and in that cycle, eventually, you will experience all of the
thousands of forms of suffering. If you do not do your
spiritual practice every day, you will experience death,
diseases, violence and thousands of types of suffering,
lifetime after lifetime. If you do your spiritual practice
every day for the maximum amount of time you can create
by dropping all unnecessary activities, eventually all forms
of suffering will end and you will live in
Infinite-Eternal-Awareness-Love-Bliss.
The purpose of spiritual practice is to experience
infinite-eternal-awareness-love-bliss in this lifetime,
not in the afterlife or some future lifetime. However,
for those who do not succeed in bringing the ego to its final
end in this imaginary lifetime, their efforts have not been
wasted because they will be much more ripe for liberation
in the next imaginary lifetime. All delays are tricks
of the ego. All detours are tricks of the impostor self.
All distractions are tricks of the false pretend self.

Every thought that leads you away from spiritual practice is a trick created by the impostor. Look at your daily activities and drop all those activities that are not necessary, to create as much time as possible for spiritual practice everyday. Bathing and eating food everyday are necessary. For most people working to earn a living everyday is necessary. Entertainment is not necessary. Make sure your spiritual practice is the most direct and rapid means to infinite-eternal-awareness-love-bliss.

You have a choice between CHOICE A:
*Infinite-Eternal-Awareness-Love-Bliss with no suffering.
*Absolutely perfect Love-Bliss for all eternity.
*Living in and knowing your true Self, eternally.

Or CHOICE B:
*Thousands of forms of suffering, sorrow, violence, diseases and death, over and over again, death-rebirth-death-rebirth-death-rebirth-death.
*Living from and knowing an impostor self.
*Living from an acquired false self (thought).
*Living from a parasite pretending to be your self.

Make CHOICE A.
Every day you do your spiritual practice,
you are making CHOICE A.
Every day you do not do your spiritual practice,
you are making CHOICE B.

Read Chapters Five and Thirteen in
The Direct Means to Eternal Bliss
and the Step Five quotes in *The Seven Steps to Awakening*
every day.
The pretend self is very tricky
and tries to lead people away from spiritual practice.
Reading Chapters Five and Thirteen every day
will help combat the ego's tricks.

Every day look at your activities
and drop all activities that are not really necessary.
Every day create as much time as possible for spiritual
practice. Do your spiritual practice every day.
Every day you have a CHOICE.
You cannot change yesterday's choices,
therefore, do not worry about yesterday's choices.
What you can do is: *Do your spiritual practice today.*

Before the extremely intense desire for Freedom
is awakened, the false self will lead you to a practice
and a teaching that will support the ego.
After the extremely intense desire for Freedom is
awakened, you will be lead to the spiritual practice that is
the most rapid means to Infinite-Eternal-Awareness-Love-
Bliss. After the extremely intense desire for Freedom is
awakened, you will be able to see how the ego has
contaminated all of the spiritual and religious teachings of
the past, including both esoteric and exoteric teachings.
Reading Chapter Five and Chapter Thirteen every day
may be enough to awaken in you
the extremely intense desire for Freedom.

Self-honesty is a great help towards awakening the
extremely intense desire for Freedom. Watch the ego
when it tries to lead you away from spiritual practice
into distractions, detours, diversions, delays, unnecessary
activities and entertainment. *Do not let the ego win that
battle.* Time is precious. A human lifespan is very short.
You have been shown the most direct and rapid means to
eternal bliss in this lifetime.   Hundreds of millions of
lifetimes may pass before you have this opportunity again.
Value every second. Don't waste a second.
Do not waste time in activities that lead
only to that which is temporary and therefore futile.
Ask of each activity, "Where can this lead?"
Ask of each activity, "Can this lead to eternal bliss,
or does this lead to that which is temporary?"

There are thousands of quotes from the spiritual teachings of the past that support the teachings in the book you are now reading. Reading the book *The Seven Steps to Awakening* repeatedly may help to awaken the extremely intense desire for Freedom. Find out what awakens the extremely intense desire for Freedom in you and do it.

Choose the Direct Experience of
infinite-eternal-*existence-being-life*, here and now
in this lifetime, by making it the first priority in your life,
and by centering your entire life on your spiritual practice.

Choose the Direct Experience of
infinite-eternal-*awareness*,
here and now in this lifetime,
by making it the first priority in your life,
and by centering your entire life on your spiritual practice.

Choose the Direct Experience of
infinite-eternal-*bliss*, here and now in this lifetime,
by making it the first priority in your life,
and by centering your entire life on your spiritual practice.

Choose the Direct Experience of
infinite-eternal-*love*, here and now in this lifetime,
by making it the first priority in your life,
and by centering your entire life on your spiritual practice.

If you find that at some point
a substantial amount of your time
has slipped back into unnecessary activities,
then you could try reading Chapter Five and Chapter
Thirteen in *The Direct Means to Eternal Bliss*
and the Step Five quotes in *The Seven Steps to Awakening*
every day until you have once again
dropped all unnecessary activities,
and are using all of the free time thus created to practice
the most direct and rapid means to eternal bliss.

If reading Chapter Five and Chapter Thirteen in *The Direct Means to Eternal Bliss* every day for a few months does not result in your dropping all unnecessary activities to free up the maximum amount of time for your spiritual practice, then you could read the entire book again, very slowly, starting with the introduction, then Chapter One, etc. If reading the Step Five quotes in *The Seven Steps to Awakening* does not awaken the extremely intense desire for Freedom in you, then you could reread that entire book.

All of the steps outlined in *The Direct Means to Eternal Bliss* from a detailed description of the impostor, to understanding how the impostor arose, seeing the difference between the impostor and the true Self, understanding the impostor's tricks, the methods used to see that thought has no real foundation, the importance of awakening the extremely intense desire for Freedom, the methods to awaken the extremely intense desire for Freedom, the Awareness Watching Awareness Method, The Abandon Release Method, The Eternal Method, The Infinite Space Method, The Loving All Method and the Loving Consciousness Method are essential for most people, due to the tricks of the ego.

What is new on a combination lock that you have been unable to open is not the numbers on the dial. What is new is the combination that opens the lock. What makes this book unique is the particular step-by-step formula or recipe described. Many of the ingredients have been mentioned in the spiritual teachings of the past. They have been mixed with ever so many non-essentials. Removing all the non-essentials and placing only the essentials into one book is one of the factors that make this book unique.
Failing to discern the difference between one spiritual teaching and another is an ego preservation strategy.

If you find some similar sentences in this book
and some of the spiritual books of the past that in no way
changes the fact that this book is quite different from
all of the spiritual books written in the past.
One fragment in one book and another fragment
in another book is not the precise formula
that is most effective for Freedom from the ego.

For example, very few spiritual books give a detailed
description of the difference between the ego and the true
Self. Of those that do, very few describe how the impostor
arose. Of those that do, very few go into detail describing
the tricks the ego uses to preserve its imaginary self.
Of those that do, very few have listed the awakening of the
extremely intense desire for Freedom as the solution to
every problem a spiritual seeker encounters,
including the trillions of tricks the ego can generate.
Of those that do, very few have given step-by-step methods
for awakening the extremely intense desire for Freedom.
Of those that do, very few have pointed out
that all of the "spiritual" teachings of the past
have been contaminated by the ego and now serve the ego.
Of those that do, very few have described
the Most Direct and Rapid Means to Eternal Bliss.

Awareness watching awareness,
which can be described in many ways such as;
awareness aware only of awareness, consciousness
conscious of consciousness, awareness aware of itself,
was taught in a very small number of the spiritual
teachings of the past.
It was ignored in those very same teachings,
buried by the ego in thousands of non-essentials.
To remove all the non-essentials and restore awareness
watching awareness to its rightful place
as the most direct and rapid means to eternal bliss is new.
That is only one fragment of this formula.

The repetition in this book is deliberate.
It is far more effective to have an insight into five points
that permanently change one's consciousness,
than to collect information about
a thousand so-called "spiritual" teachings
and remain as a sleeping egotist.

Making a simple spiritual teaching into
something complicated is a trick generated by the ego.
Thus, communicating only the essentials
in simple plain language is quite deliberate in this book.
Similar words will usually not produce the same results.
The new wording in this book, that leaves out the
non-essentials and points directly to the essentials,
can produce very different results.
Failure to discern the differences between one spiritual
teaching and another is an ego preservation strategy.

Reading this book at different times in your life
can produce different results.
If, even after reading this book many times,
the ego did not allow you to see the value of what is here,
try reading the book again a few months or a year from
now or when your openness or desire for Freedom
has increased.

For those of you who have reached the point where
you have dropped all unnecessary activities to create the
maximum amount of time to practice the most direct and
rapid means to eternal bliss, if you choose to add
something, the recommendation would be to add the
Loving All Method. All of the methods in the book
except the Loving All Method are to be practiced
when there are no other activities going on.
The Loving All Method
can be practiced during all activities.
Thus the Loving All Method is a means to
use all of your time productively towards your awakening.

For thousands of years humans have passed a nightmare world full of suffering, lies, deceit, fear, anger, and violence unto their children. To stop this cycle: challenge the assumptions, ideas, beliefs and concepts that were taught to you at a young age and now form the basis for your perceptions.

Although it was suggested that you suspend doubt long enough to see what is presented in this book, you need not suspend doubt forever.
Doubt is a very valuable tool in the process of awakening.
You could begin by doubting all of the religious and spiritual teachings of the past.
See how those teachings are serving the ego.
Then doubt every human belief in all fields including science and philosophy.
See how all those thoughts and beliefs are serving the ego.
Then doubt the validity, sincerity and existence of the doubter. Find out: who or what is the doubter?

Then practice the most direct and rapid means to eternal bliss. Then, eventually, sooner or later, experience the absolute perfection of Infinite-Eternal-Awareness-Love-Bliss.
Then continue to practice.

For this to happen you have to begin to care.
Care about Truth enough to see that the human past has been a falsehood.
Care about Truth enough to drop the past ideas, beliefs, concepts and opinions.
Then begin a new life.

Read Chapter 13 very slowly three times before reading Chapter 14.

CHAPTER FOURTEEN

EXPERIENCES, THE JOURNEY

AND THE FINAL GOAL

Many spiritual teachings have maps or lists of stages or signs of progress. For a teaching that has as its goal bringing the impostor self to its final end all such maps or lists are false. There are no uniform signs or stages. One aspirant may have a very noisy mind two moments before the ego's final end, then one moment of silence, then the ego's final end.
Another aspirant may have a long extended period of silence before the ego's final end. One way to understand this is to take the example of a dream or of sleep.
What are the signs or indications that you are waking up from a dream or from sleep?
There may be such signs, but they differ not only from person to person but even from dream to dream. By the time you are aware of a sign, the next moment you are awake. Otherwise, you are just dreaming. Either you are dreaming or you are not dreaming. Either you are sleeping or you are awake.
The notion of signs of progress towards awakening is not valid and not helpful to the aspirant. A thousand different experiences may happen during your years of spiritual practice. Whatever sign there may be that the ego is about to come to its final end may only be known to you the moment before the ego comes to its final end. Thus being concerned with signs of progress during your years of practice is not helpful or valid. Progress may be imperceptible to the practitioner. A turbulent state can be a sign of progress if you are in the stage of doing battle with the ego. A peaceful state can be a sign of progress.

The most helpful view for the aspirant is not to be
concerned with signs of progress. If a list were given
that was supposed to describe signs of progress, those who
were not experiencing those signs would be discouraged.
Such a list would be false. The human dream is a delusion.
Looking for signs of progress in a delusion is an error.

Almost all experiences during spiritual practice
are illusions. Thus to look towards illusions
for signs of progress towards awakening is folly.
This is true regardless of whether those illusions are
blissful or sad. When a list of signs of progress is not
given, what the aspirant has to fall back on is:
What was it that gave the aspirant the confidence
that the method they are practicing
is the most rapid and direct means to eternal bliss?
In the case of the Awareness Watching Awareness Method,
it is the fact that one's attention is focused exclusively
on the background of awareness
that makes it the most direct and rapid means.
In other words, your true Self is awareness.
The most rapid and direct means to
the direct perception of your awareness is your awareness.
That makes it the most direct practice
with no distractions or detours.

Your first year of practice might be mostly
turbulence. Your second year of practice might be mostly
peaceful or blissful. Or your first year of practice might be
mostly peaceful or blissful and your second year of practice
might be mostly turbulent.

At some point the ego tries to stop the practice
or progress of most people. The ego can do this at almost
any time, even after someone has been practicing for years.
That is one reason why half of this book
has been devoted to exposing the ego, the ego's tricks,
and how to reduce and finally end those tricks.
100

The solution is the awakening of the extremely intense desire for Freedom. Some people do not pay much attention to chapter's One through Five and go directly to the Awareness Watching Awareness practice. That may or may not work out well for them. Having a firm foundation by awakening the extremely intense desire for Freedom and maintaining that desire everyday helps to solve all obstacles and also makes the practice more effective. Therefore, from time to time reread chapters One through Five.

EXPERIENCES

There are trillions of possibilities regarding what you might experience while engaged in spiritual practice. Almost everything you experience during your spiritual practice should be ignored. Some notable exceptions are if you have symptoms of a heart attack such as chest pains, etc. you should stop practicing and immediately call an ambulance. If your smoke detector sounds its alarm, you should stop practicing and make sure there is no fire in your house. With the exceptions of those events which are an emergency or extremely urgent, almost everything else in the environment, body and inner experience should be ignored during your practice sessions.

The goal is to perceive the seer. Almost any experience you have, including those you consider to be spiritual experiences, are the seen and not the seer. They are the perceived, not the perceiver. Therefore, they should be ignored. Experiences can be created from the power of suggestion. Two different spiritual groups, who as part of a spiritual teaching are taught that they can expect two different kinds of spiritual experiences, will tend to have experiences that match what they have been told to expect, even if they are practicing the same method.

This is an example of the power of suggestion.
This is also an example of the power of illusion.
It should not be a surprise to you that the mind can create
an experience from the power of suggestion
since it is now presenting the illusion to you that there is
a planet called earth where there is in fact no such planet.
This same principle applies to the universe, etc.
Give people a list of the signs of spiritual progress
and the mind can create such experiences.
Unless the ego wants them to move onto a different
practice or teaching in which case the ego may be
unwilling to produce such experiences.

Whatever you experience during spiritual practice,
ignore it and turn your attention away from it and towards
the background of awareness. Turn your attention away
from the seen and towards the seer. Turn your attention
away from the known and towards the knower. Turn your
attention away from the heard and towards the hearer.

You may experience a place, a realm, or another
dimension. The place may have entities in it. It may seem
to be the most wonderful, loving, beautiful place you have
ever seen. Ignore it. All realms, all places, all dimensions
and all entities are temporary illusions. The Reality is not
a place and has no places in it. Thus even if you manage to
live what seems like a trillion earth years in what seems to
be a beautiful wonderful realm or place, it will come to an
end. Then you will be right back in the cycle of births and
deaths. For example: one hundred million imaginary
lifetimes of suffering in realms that are not pleasant.

There may be entities in the beautiful realms
that try and convince you that those realms are eternal.
Don't believe those entities. No place is eternal.
No realm is eternal. All realms and all places
had a beginning in time and will have an end in time.

Keep in mind that you may never experience any realm or place or entity.

That which is temporary is not the goal.
That which is temporary will not free you from sorrow.
With any temporary experience, including a very blissful experience, you will end up right back where you started from – with suffering. Temporary happiness, temporary bliss, temporary love, or temporary peace will not free you. A temporary experience will not free you.

A temporary entity or place may seem to help, however; in the end they will not have produced any real help. It is best to ignore all that you experience during spiritual practice by turning your attention away from the experience and towards the experiencer.

THE FINAL GOAL

What is the goal of practice? It is to bring the impostor self and its suffering and illusions to a final end so that only the true Self whose nature is Infinite-Eternal-Awareness-Love-Bliss remains. When the impostor self comes to its final end the perception of the world and the universe also come to a final end. You can read about that in the Step Two quotes in *The Seven Steps to Awakening*. You can read about what remains in the Step Five quotes in *The Seven Steps to Awakening*.

What is most important is already described in the paragraph above. An attempt will be made to describe the final goal further; however, such descriptions are not what is most important. The fact that when the impostor self ends, all suffering ends for all eternity and that the True Self has never had any suffering in all eternity and is always absolutely perfect love-bliss is what is most important.

Suppose you try to describe the taste of pineapple juice to someone who has never tasted it. You say it is both sweet and tart at the same time. There are many juices that are both sweet and tart and none of them taste like pineapple juice. Thus you have failed to convey the taste through words. If one cannot convey the taste of pineapple juice through words, how can the final Reality be described through words since the final Reality is not within the human frame of reference?

Describing the final Reality as
Infinite-Eternal-Awareness-Love-Bliss
is the closest one can come in words
without straying too far from the human frame of reference. In the final Reality, which is the only Reality, there are no worlds, no places, no dimensions, no universe, no realms, no forms, no time, no things, no beings and almost nothing
that any word in the dictionary points towards.
In the final Reality, which is the only Reality, there are no humans, no animals, no planets, no stars, and no earth.

The final Reality is infinite awareness aware only of infinite awareness. The final Reality, which is the only Reality, is infinite awareness aware of itself and itself is infinite awareness. In all of eternity the final Reality has never been aware of anything other than infinite awareness-love-bliss. Awareness-love-bliss are not three, it is one. In all of eternity the final Reality, which is the true Self, has never been aware of a human, or a world or suffering of any kind. Humans, animals, earth, planets, stars, other realms, entities, places, time, dimensions, and that which almost every word in the dictionary points towards is part of the ego dream.
When the ego comes to its final end, the dream ends and almost everything that the words in the dictionary point towards disappears.
104

When the ego comes to its final end, what remains is Infinite-Eternal-Awareness-Love-Bliss and nothing ever reappears. The planets, the stars, and almost everything that the words in the dictionary point towards never reappear. They were all part of the dream.
Upon awakening, the dream disappears.
The state humans consider to be their real life, the state that occurs when they wake up from sleep is a type of dream. You could call it the waking-dream. The type of dream that occurs when humans are sleeping could be called the sleeping-dream. There are many differences between the waking-dream and the sleeping-dream. For example there is a sense of continuity in the waking-dream. Humans wake up into the story where the story left off. When the ego comes to its final end, both the waking-dream and the sleeping-dream end. When the ego comes to its final end,
there is no longer the perception of a body or a world. That is not the same as saying the body dies. If you go to sleep tonight and dream of flying camels, when you wake up the flying camels did not die. They just disappeared. Suppose you have a friend named Joe. Suppose that Joe is one of those rare one in millions of humans who succeeds in ending the ego illusion. From the moment of the ending of the ego illusion Joe no longer has any perception of a body or a world. Yet from your perspective, assuming you are one who is still dreaming the human dream,
you will still perceive Joe's body functioning normally. You will see Joe walking, talking, eating and going about daily activities. An example to make this clearer is sleepwalking. Sleepwalkers may get up from the bed, go to the refrigerator, grab a glass of milk, and drink the glass of milk all while remaining asleep. The state of the one who has ended the ego is not identical with sleepwalking; this example is provided because the human mind tends to start with the assumption that the sage's body only being perceptible to a third party onlooker is something incomprehensible.

Here is yet another example. There are two friends named Sally and Joe. Joe is an astronaut. Joe takes a ship to the moon. Sally goes to sleep at night and has a dream. In the dream she is talking to Joe. But Joe is really on the moon. Therefore, even though Sally sees Joe walking and talking and sees Joe still living on the earth in her dream, Joe is not really on the earth. This also is just an example to attempt to make something more comprehensible that humans find difficult to comprehend. The awakened sage has not gone to some other place. In the case of an awakened sage the dream has ended that contained the place. Both the sleeping-dream and the waking-dream have ended for the awakened sage.

Often when a human wakes up from a sleeping-dream, they have no memory of the sleeping-dream. Or they have a memory only for a minute or so upon awakening and then they cannot remember their sleeping-dream. The sage who has awakened from both the sleeping-dream and the waking-dream has no memory of ever having been human. Yet to one who is still dreaming it will *appear* that the sage is still carrying on normal physical life. The sage will *appear* to be talking, eating, etc. The one still dreaming creates a waking-dream that includes the appearance of the body of the awakened sage.

When you go to sleep at night and have a sleeping-dream all that appears in your sleeping-dream is just your own consciousness. All the people you communicate with and all the places are really just your own consciousness. They are not real. They are your consciousness appearing as people, places, events and things. Therefore what they really are is just one consciousness that has the ability to appear as everything in the dream.
106

The example just given applies to the waking-dream also. Everything you perceive in the waking-dream, which is what humans mistakenly call real life, is one consciousness that has the ability to appear as the earth, people, animals, plants, stars, etc. In other words one consciousness that has the ability to appear as everything including almost everything that the words in the dictionary point towards.
That one consciousness appears as both things and actions.

There is a description that is even closer to the truth of the final Reality. That is that the final Reality never appears as the earth, humans or almost anything that the words in the dictionary point towards. The final Reality always remains as it is and there has never been a human, planet or almost anything the words in the dictionary point towards in the final Reality.

One can use the example of a movie theatre. In some places this may be called cinema. The light inside the light bulb in the projector represents the final Reality or in other words the True Self. The film represents thoughts, feelings, emotions, the body, the five senses, etc. On the screen a world is seen. However, inside the light which is inside the light bulb inside the projector there is no world, no movie, no people etc.

All of what is described here can be known in direct experience by bringing the ego to its final end.

The difference between the deep dreamless sleep state and the final Reality is that in the deep dreamless sleep state there appears to be unconsciousness.
In the final Reality there is awareness that never changes and is always aware.

When you wake up from a sleeping-dream,
where did the world and people you dreamed about go?
They did not go anywhere.
They were never really there
even while you were dreaming.
So it is when you wake up from the human waking-dream.
The planets, people, animals, plants, stars, etc.
were never really there.
They seemed real while you were dreaming them
in the waking-dream,
just like what you experience in the sleeping-dream
seems real while you are dreaming it.
When you wake up from the waking-dream,
which happens when the ego comes to its final end,
the planets, people, animals, plants, stars, etc. disappear,
similar to how whatever you dream in the sleeping-dream
disappears upon your waking up.

Imagine an ocean of consciousness.
Instead of an ocean of water,
this is an ocean of consciousness.
Almost all of the waves on this ocean of consciousness
have developed the habit of never looking down.
They only look out horizontally.
Because they only look out horizontally all they see are
what appears to be billions of separate waves.
They assume that there is no ocean,
only separate waves.
One day one of these waves has the courage
to dive deep down within itself and discovers the ocean.
This wave discovers that there is no line
that separates it from the ocean.
This wave discovers that there are no waves,
there is only the ocean.
Wave is a concept created by imagining there is
a bottom line that separates the wave from the ocean.
There are no waves, there is only the ocean.
This can be known in direct experience.
108

SPIRITUAL PRACTICE

Because the true Self is eternally perfect awareness-love-bliss and eternally free of all suffering, some people think there is no need for spiritual practice. Such a notion is an ego preservation strategy. The purpose of practice is not to gain the true Self. The purpose of practice is to remove the illusion of a body, a world, suffering, etc. so that what remains is only the eternal experience of the True Self. In other words, those who have let the ego trick them into thinking there is no need for spiritual practice, because the True Self is eternally free of suffering, etc., are still having the experience of suffering, a body, a world, etc. Thus their experience is not consistent with the fact that the True Self is eternally free of suffering and perfectly blissful. This is an example of intellectual "spirituality." This is an example of people confusing a journey through concepts, ideas, beliefs and opinions with an authentic spiritual journey. Practice leads to the direct experience of Infinite-Eternal-Awareness-Love-Bliss. A journey through spiritual concepts, ideas, beliefs, teachings and opinions is a journey through illusion. Practice is what is essential. It must not be a spiritual practice that is created by the ego for the purpose of preserving the ego. In the book *The Importance of Practice & Effort* the Seven Sages describe why practice is essential.

With the Awareness Watching Awareness Method, the practice is the progress. The habit has been developed of always looking outward towards the seen. The Awareness Watching Awareness Method reverses this. Every time a thought arises, or the tendency to look outward, the attention is taken away from the thought and turned towards the seer. Thus with the Awareness Watching Awareness Method a new habit is developed and the practice is the progress.

A question might arise why does the Awareness Watching Awareness Method focus attention on one's ordinary everyday background of awareness instead of attempting to look for Infinite Awareness?

Here is an example that can answer this question:

Imagine that you live in a mansion that has thousands of dark rooms and you are trying to find the sunlight.

If you focus your attention on a beam of sunlight that enters one of the rooms and follow that beam and trace its origin you can find the source of that light – the Sun.

However, if you hold the concept of the Sun and ignore the beam of sunlight that enters some of the rooms, you could open a thousand doors in dark rooms and never find the Sun.

In this example the Sun represents the Infinite Awareness which is the True Self. The beam of sunlight represents your ordinary everyday consciousness.

If people hold some concept of infinite awareness and try to find it, they will never find it.

Your own everyday background of awareness is the path to Infinite Awareness, as a beam of sunlight is to the Sun.

Another example:

Imagine a planet where all of the people were born and raised and spent their entire lives in a movie theatre. Almost all of them believed the movie they were seeing on the screen was real. Their attention was so fixed on the screen that they never bothered to turn their heads around 180 degrees to see the projector's light.

One of them had the courage to turn his head around 180 degrees and he saw the projector's light.

He did not know what it was, but he followed that light until he found the projector. He went back and told the people that what they were seeing on the screen was not real. He told them that to find the projector they would have to turn their heads around 180 degrees.

110

Due to the long habit of always keeping their attention
fixed on the movie screen, fear of the unknown,
their belief that the movie was real,
and their disbelief in what he was telling them,
very few bothered to turn their heads around 180 degrees
to see the light from the projector.
Some of those who did follow his instructions
turned their heads immediately back to the screen.
They were used to the illusion and afraid of the Truth.
Others did not sustain their attempt to find the projector
long enough to find it.
After all it is difficult to find the projector in the dark.
One has to pass through a number of doors to find it.
Once in a while someone actually persevered long enough
to find the projector.

     If you are in a dark room, spiritual practice is like
opening the drapes or curtains. If a person says the Sun is
there, therefore there is no need to open the drapes,
that person will always live in darkness. So it is with those
who say there is no need for spiritual practice.
There was a spiritual teacher who for more than fifty years
gave talks around the world.
He said there is no need for practice.
He said any movement of the me center (ego)
helps to perpetuate the me center.
That might sound logical; however, what are the actual
results? Towards the end of his life it was this teacher's
view that none of the people who had attended his talks
or read his books had succeeded in ending the me center.
Practice is essential. Talking you out of spiritual practice
is an ego preservation strategy.
There is another way to understand the need for practice:
Most of the people of the world are not doing any spiritual
practice. This no-practice is not leading any of them to the
Final Awakening, the final end of all suffering and illusion.
Thus it is essential to find a practice that is effective,
and then to actually do the practice every day.

THE LOVING CONSCIOUSNESS METHOD

This is a primary method meaning that it is to be practiced every day for as many hours per day as you can create by dropping all unnecessary activities. The preliminary instructions are the same as for the Awareness Watching Awareness Method and the definition of Awareness and Consciousness is the same also. See Chapter Seven for both.

PRACTICE INSTRUCTIONS
FOR THE LOVING CONSCIOUSNESS METHOD

Shut your eyes. Love your consciousness. Continue to feel love towards your awareness throughout the practice session. Worship your consciousness. Cherish your consciousness. Value your consciousness. If the instructions to worship, cherish and value your consciousness do not convey any meaning that you can put into practice then you can ignore those instructions and just use the instructions to feel love towards your consciousness. Your awareness loving your awareness. What makes this simple practice unique is the way awareness and consciousness are defined in this book. In this practice you are not loving thoughts, feelings, etc. You are loving the background of awareness. You can find more detailed instructions for how to practice The Loving Consciousness Method in the book *How to Live a Life that Knows Only Love.* There are 26 descriptions of the Loving Consciousness Method in that book. The book *How to Live a Life that Knows Only Love* has quotes about Love by 10 authors that support both the Loving Consciousness Method and The Loving All Method.

The question may arise which of the three primary practices, the Awareness Watching Awareness Method, the Abandon Release Method or the Loving Consciousness Method should you practice?

Try practicing the Awareness Watching Awareness Method first. Practice it for as long as the ego will allow you to practice it. If the ego will allow you to practice it permanently then continue to practice the Awareness Watching Awareness Method.

If the ego tries to stop you from practicing whatever method you are practicing, try to persevere. If the ego wins the battle and you stop practicing the Awareness Watching Awareness Method, then try practicing the Abandon Release Method. If the ego stops you from practicing the Abandon Release Method, then try practicing the Loving Consciousness Method. Do not confuse the Loving All Method with the Loving Consciousness Method. They are different Methods.

Hopefully you can practice each method for at least one year before moving onto another method. That way you can gain some skill with the method. You can continue to practice the method you like best. Or, if you tire of one method you could try alternating, practicing the Awareness Watching Awareness Method for one year, then switching to the Abandon Release Method for the second year, then for the third year switching to the Loving Consciousness Method, then for the fourth year back to the Awareness Watching Awareness Method. All three methods are complimentary. In other words skill in one of the methods helps to develop skill in the other methods.

The question may arise who or what does the practice? It is the ego that leads one to practice. Usually the ego leads one to practice a method that will allow the ego to continue. Thus the human delusion and human evil continues. However, it is possible for the ego to see the need for its own end. Chapter Five reveals many ways to show the ego the need for its own end.

One of the most important of these is the exercise to face the ocean of human suffering, sorrow, deceit, cruelty etc. Usually humans only face a few drops in that ocean. Usually humans block that ocean from their awareness. Thus the extent of human evil, or in other words the ego's evil, is not seen. A human might be willing to look at part of one war. However it is very rare that a human is willing to look at what fifteen thousand wars in the last five thousand years really means. Seeing what happened to each and every individual human in those wars. In addition to the wars, trillions of acts of violence have occurred. Billions of lies are told by humans each and every day including today. Billions of acts of cruelty occur every day including today. Yet all this is still only a few drops in the ocean of human suffering and evil. This is a case where a picture is worth a thousand words. Photographs of human bodies after the acts of violence have occurred can convey much more than mere words. Billions of acts of verbal deceit, conning, and cheating occur every day including today. Humans lie not only to each other but to themselves every day.

There is a further step one can take to see the extent of the ego's vast network of deception, cruelty, insincerity, etc. That is to see how usually what humans call good is also the ego's evil in a hidden form.

The capacity of thought is tremendous. All of the information in all of the books that have ever been written has been created by thought. All of the information on the entire World Wide Web has been created by thought. All the technology from going to the moon to computers, etc. has been created by thought. Even in one single human the possible combinations that thought, ideas, concepts, etc. can take number in the trillions. If human thought were basically something sincere with good pure motives, life would be quite different.

114

However, thought is not something basically sincere with good pure motives. Thought is something insincere and deceptive with sinister motives. Thought has thousands of layers of self deception. When something that is basically deceptive and dishonest has such a vast network of thought to work with, it is not difficult to see how thought has been able to keep almost all humans prisoner for all of human history. Seeing the extent of the self-deception, thought's layer upon layer of self-deception, dishonesty, insincerity and thought's ability
to hide what it is doing from its imaginary self,
is the key to understanding the ancient human trap.
It is also the key to understanding how all of the religious and spiritual teachings of the past serve the ego.
Thought hides its true nature.
Thought blocks out its sinister, deceptive nature
and pretends to itself that it is sincere and good.
That which has produced 15,000 wars in the last 5,000 years and trillions of lies is not sincere and good.

Self honesty begins by beginning to face the insincerity, deceptiveness, evil and cruelty of thought.
Progress in self honesty is seeing that the extent of thought's insincerity, deceptiveness, evil and cruelty
is much vaster than one ever suspected. Something like going through one's life thinking that a lake of insincerity, deceptiveness, evil and cruelty was the extent of it
and discovering that the network of thought was not a lake but an ocean of insincerity, deceptiveness, evil and cruelty.
It is important to see this ocean both in other humans and in one's own mind also. See the vast network of thought.
If one does a good job of seeing this, then statements such as "All the spiritual teachings of the past serve the ego"
will not seem like too strong a statement. The ego
has not left the spiritual teachings of the past untouched.
The ego has made sure that the spiritual and religious teachings of the past serve the ego.

If you face the ocean of human evil and suffering,
including the more than fifteen thousand wars
in the last five thousand years, you can see that humans
are delusional. The spiritual and religious teachings of the
past are a product of that same delusion. It is not only
religious or spiritual thought that serves the ego.
Almost all human thought serves the ego. By looking at
the results, i.e. the history of human evil, one can see that
is true. It is not one little isolated event of cruelty,
deception, insincerity etc.,
it is trillions of acts of cruelty, deception, insincerity, etc.

One reason why it is so important to become aware
of the ocean of human suffering, deception, insincerity,
cruelty, etc. is because that is one of the steps towards
ending it. The very fact that humans pretend that human
insincerity is not omnipresent is one of the factors that has
always allowed human insincerity to flourish. Making
excuses and creating explanations, rationalizations,
and justifications for human evil has been one of the
primary factors that has allowed human evil to continue.
If one sees and rejects all those excuses, explanations,
rationalizations and justifications and instead just sees
human evil as evil, that is a first step towards the ending of
human evil. If you do not like the word evil you can use
the words cruelty, deception, hurtfulness, harmfulness,
lying, cheating, conning, violence (both physical and
verbal), insincerity, dishonesty, pretense, apathy, hatred.

Suppose there is a man who considers himself to be
very logical, rational and scientifically minded.
This man rejects all the religious and spiritual teachings.
He thinks he is a body and when the body dies that is the
end of it. Therefore, whatever pleasure he can get out of
this brief material life is in his view the purpose of his life.
The spiritual teachings of the past have stated that there is
more to what a human is than just his body-mind. They
have stated that the true nature of the human is eternal.

It is understandable that the man has rejected those
spiritual teachings that rely on belief to establish this,
and that state that one will find the truth of this when the
body dies, because those teachings are a distortion of the
original teachings of the founders of those religions,
and are changes made to those teachings for
religious-political or religious-business reasons.
However, there are also the experiential spiritual teachings
that are not relying on beliefs. They say do such and such
a practice and you can experience the results.   Now this
man has a choice. He is offered the possibility of eternal
perfect love-bliss or a temporary brief life and death.
If this man were truly rational, logical, sane, etc. the
potential gain is so great he would make the decision to do
a spiritual practice that can reveal to him his true Self
and thus live eternally in love-bliss free of all suffering.
However, he holds the belief that there is no such eternal
true Self. He does not know there is no eternal true Self.
He just believes there is no eternal true Self.
He is not rational, logical or sane, although he believes
he is rational, logical and sane. What is it that leads him
to the decision not to do a spiritual practice that has the
potential to reveal to him his true Self and let him enter
the ocean of eternal bliss? It is the ego. The pro-religious
believer, and the anti-religious disbeliever who thinks he is
so rational, are both lost in belief. Belief is not Truth.

If somehow the ego allows either the one who
believes or the one who disbelieves in the True Self
to see the great value in becoming a knower,
which is of course not a believer or a disbeliever, then
there are a huge number of practices that they could try.
There are Hindu, Buddhist, Christian Mysticism,
and Sufi practices. There are also practices
that do not fall within such popular categories.
Explaining in detail why all such practices do not lead to
the ego's final end and how all such teachings and
practices serve the ego would require a large book.

However, when one names specific teachings and begins to list the defects in those teachings and how they serve the ego, many people tend to have a strong emotional reaction because of their attachment to and investment in such beliefs. Thus it is more helpful to point out the quotes from those traditions that do not serve the ego.
Also, even if one points out the defects etc.,
if the extremely intense desire for Truth
and Freedom is not there
they will not see what is being pointed out.

If the desire for Truth and Freedom is great enough the aspirant can see how the spiritual teachings of the past serve the ego without it being pointed out to them. Ask the question: How does this spiritual teaching serve the ego? Then examine the spiritual teaching
to find the answer to that question.

Different spiritual teachings have different goals. The ego likes a goal that is at least somewhat familiar to it. The ego wants its dream to continue, therefore most people will block out any teaching aimed at ending the dream of a universe. If one examines very carefully the religious and spiritual teachings of the past one can see that they are perpetuating evil and perpetuating the impostor self. The impostor self usually does not allow people to see that fact. One can look at how religious ideas are spread. Usually people are taught beliefs of a particular religion from childhood. Read books about Memes or Memetics to learn more about how religious and other beliefs are spread from human to human much like a virus. Thus the beliefs of a particular religion become a basic part of the person's mind. There is usually a lifetime bias towards the religion the person was taught.
Sometimes the religion contains terrible threats of eternal punishment. Thus the person can no longer see clearly the evil that the religion or spiritual teaching is perpetuating.

Human thought can always find an explanation or justification for evil. If every time thought tries to explain evil away you do not believe the explanations but instead just say no to the evil, then everything will start to change for you. You would then walk away from such a religion or spiritual teaching and never return.

Suppose you go to sleep tonight and have a dream. In that dream one thousand scientists present ten thousand pages of evidence to support a certain conclusion. Maybe for example the conclusion that everything experienced in meditation including the most profound experiences are created by the brain. When you wake up from the dream you find that the scientists and all their evidence were just a dream and their evidence and conclusions you now know had no validity. While dreaming the dream seems real.

Science can be very helpful to navigate the waking-dream and make the waking-dream less painful. If your body has symptoms of illness, go to see a modern medical doctor. Where science fails is in being helpful with waking up from the waking-dream. The ego in the scientist is just as dedicated to continuing the waking-dream as is the ego in the religious believer, the philosopher and almost all other human beings. There are current scientific discoveries that support the notion that all is one consciousness. However, science is constantly changing. In the year three thousand, the views of science of the year two thousand will be thought to be absurd. In the year four thousand the views of science of the year three thousand will be thought to be absurd. Science is for the purpose of discovering that which is relatively truer. Science is not for the purpose of experiencing the Absolute Truth that has never changed in all eternity and that will never change in all eternity.

The ego only pretends to want Freedom,
except in very rare cases.
Therefore, the religious person is not seeking Freedom
and the experience of the Infinite-Awareness.
The religious person is only pretending to themselves
that they want eternal Freedom-Bliss-Love.
The scientist is only pretending to want Truth.
Almost all humans serve the false ego.
Suppose someone begins the study and practice
of a spiritual or religious teaching.
Thought says "I am sincere; I really intend to attain the
goal of this teaching." However, there is another deeper
layer of thought that knows it really has no intention of
ever attaining the goal of the spiritual teaching.
Thus the aspirants imagine they are sincere
when in fact they are not sincere.
That is an example of self-deception.
Self-honesty is the cure.
Self-honesty begins by actually becoming aware
of the layers upon layers of self-deception.
Devote your life to Truth and Freedom.

It is not all gloomy and bleak.
There is something wonderful and extremely beautiful.
You can wake up and live eternally in
Infinite-Awareness-Love-Bliss,
free of all suffering.
Your true Self is that now.
Wishing you success in bringing the impostor (ego)
to its final end.

Start the day with love.
Fill the day with love.
End the day with love.
Treat every human and animal you come into contact with
with tenderness, kindness, care, love and gentleness.

Please use the contact form at seeseer.com to let us know if reading The Direct Means to Eternal Bliss was a good experience for you.

These are eight books which support and work well with the teachings in The Direct Means to Eternal Bliss:

1. The Seven Steps to Awakening.

2. Self Abidance, abridged edition.

3. How to practice Self Inquiry.

4. Powerful Quotes from Sankara.

5. Experience Your Perfect Soul.

6. How to Practice the Teachings is a book about how to put into practice the teachings in the books The Direct Means to Eternal Bliss and The Seven Steps to Awakening. It will be published late in 2015.

7. How to Live a Life that Knows Only Love. Will be published late in 2015.

8. The Importance of Practice & Effort. Will be published in 2016.

For information about these and other spiritual books go to:

www.seeseer.com

Made in the USA
Monee, IL
19 January 2021